THE
MANY
RIDES
OF
Paul Revere

A New Plan of ye Great Town of BOSTON in New Eng

With the many Additionall Buildings, & New Streets, to the Yea

To His Excellency Jonathan Belcher &c.
Capt. General and Governour in Chief
of His Majesties Provinces of
the Massachusets Bay & New
Hampshire in New England
and Vice Admiral of the same
this Plan of the great Town
of BOSTON is humbly
dedicated by Yor Excellencies
most obedient & humble Serv
William Price

BOSTON the Metropolis of New England, is the largest, most populous and flourishing Town in the British Dominions North, and 76 Deg West from London. It Stands at the Bottom of a large Bay, Which (by being defended from ye dreadfull Islands) May be rekon'd among the safest and most Commodious Harbours in the World. At the Entrance and about 1 League toward the Town, a Strong Castle Mounted with about 118 Cannon. The Country round about with all Sorts of good Provisions, and all other Necessaries of Life. The Air is exceeding clear & Pleasant, Perfectly in Constitution. This Town hath been Settled 104 Years, its Number of Houses about 4000 and Inhabitants about 1800.
10 Congregational Meeting Houses, 1 French, 1 Anabaptist, 1 Irish 1 Quakers Meeting House, And a very handsom Town House, where the Courts are held. The Town and Country daily increasing. In the Year 1735 were built in New England above 40 Sail of Ships and other Vessells, Most of which are fitted at Boston. There are in one Year cleard out of this Port at the Custom House, about 200 Sail of Vessells which may in some Measure shew the great Trade of this flourishing Town and Country, in the Year 1735, this Town was Divided into 12 Wards, By a Vote of the Inhabitants the bounds of the Wards are the great Lines from No. 1 to 12, in each Ward is a Militia Company of foot & a Captain &c. Also one Overseer of the Poor chosen Yearly in March.
Boston was first Settled in ye Year 1630

Printed for & Sold by Wm Price at ye Kings Head & Looking Glass in Cornhill, Near the Town House in Boston, Where is Sold a Large New South East Prospect of Boston Neatly done. A Prospect of the Colledg s in Cambridge New England. And Great Variety of Mapps & Prints of all sorts in Frames & Glass or without. Also Pictures Painted in Oyls Carved Gilt Frames Likewise for Sconces and frames all Sorts & Sizes. Newest fashion'd Looking Glasses, Tea Tables, China Ware. English & Dutch Toys for Children, by Wholesale or Retail, at Reasonable Rates.
The this hand Points to the Kings Head & Looking Glass in Cornhill.
Also Flutes, Hautboys & Violins, Strings, Musical Books, Rings, Spectacles, Prospect Glasses &c.

The Names of the 12 Wards,
New ster Street Ward
ith St Ditto
e St Ditto
nd Ward
over Ditto
bridge D
ngs St D.
hill D.
brough D.
mor St D.
age St D.

FoxHill

Powder House
Watch House

COMMON

The Town Green

School

No. 7
No. 9
No. 9
Beacon Hill

The Mall

Scale of ½ a Mile.

BOSTON, N.E. EXPLANATION.
Note the first letter of the name of the Streets is set to the bounds of Each Street

Hills Wharf
& Salt House

Wind Mill Point

Tileston's Land
Pleasant Street
Milleys Lane
Tiley's Lane
Frog Lane
No. 10
Common Street
Clough Street
No. 10
Orange Str
No. 10
Orange Str
No. 12
No. 12
No. 11
Great Wharf

From Town H
one Mile
No. 8
Orange Str
No. 12
Fortification

Other Illustrated Biographies
about Colonial American Heroes
by James Cross Giblin

George Washington: A Picture Book Biography

Thomas Jefferson: A Picture Book Biography

The Amazing Life of Benjamin Franklin

THE
MANY
RIDES
OF
Paul Revere

JAMES
CROSS
GIBLIN

SCHOLASTIC INC.
New York Toronto London Auckland Sydney
Mexico City New Delhi Hong Kong Buenos Aires

Illustrated with Archival Photographs

ISBN-13: 978-0-545-12968-8
ISBN-10: 0-545-12968-0

Text copyright © 2007 by James Cross Giblin. All rights reserved. Published by Scholastic Inc. SCHOLASTIC and associated logos are trademarks and/or registered trademarks of Scholastic Inc.

12 11   16 17 18/0

Printed in the U.S.A.   40

First Scholastic paperback printing, January 2009

The text was set in Hoefler Text.
The display type was set in Historical Fell Type.
Book design by Richard Amari

Special Thanks to Els Rijper and Allen Gottlieb from Scholastic's photo research department for their tenacious work in tracking down the art. And to Patrick Leehey, Research Director of the Paul Revere House, for his astute, meticulous, and generous consultation and fact-checking of the manuscript and pictures.

Pictured on the dedication page opposite
is Paul Revere's hallmark, which he stamped
into the objects he crafted.

*A*gain for Dianne Hess,
who makes beautiful books

REVERE

*S*pecial thanks to my friend, Russell Freedman,
who suggested that I write about Paul Revere

CONTENTS

In an attempt to make France an all-Catholic country, French Protestants, known as Huguenots, were persecuted starting in the 1680s. Here a Protestant father bids a reluctant farewell to his family before being led away by his Catholic captors. To escape such persecution, many Protestants, like young Apollos Rivoire, left France.

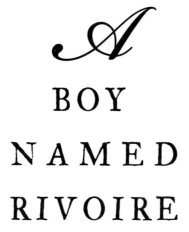BOY NAMED RIVOIRE

I F THINGS HAD BEEN DIFFERENT, HIS NAME WOULDN'T have been Paul Revere. It might have been Apollos Rivoire, like the name of his French father. But when Apollos was thirteen, his parents decided to send their son to live with his uncle Simon on the English island of Guernsey. Catholics in France were persecuting Protestants like the Rivoires, and his father and mother feared for young Apollos's safety.

This view of Boston in 1743 is similar to the one young Apollos Rivoire must have seen when he arrived in the city by boat in 1716.

Apollos didn't stay long on Guernsey, however. Uncle Simon thought there would be more opportunities for his nephew in the new land of America. And so, late in 1715, he gave Apollos a little money and put him aboard a ship that was bound for the port of Boston in far-off Massachusetts. The boy arrived in his new home on a wintry January day in 1716. He had no friends or relatives in Boston, and knew only a few words of English.

It didn't take long for him to get settled, though. The captain of the ship he had traveled on was responsible for placing young passengers like Apollos as apprentices to merchants and craftsmen. He found Apollos a place with a well-known Boston goldsmith, John Coney. Mr. Coney promised to feed and clothe Apollos, and teach him to make useful and beautiful objects of gold and silver. In return, Apollos promised to stay with Mr. Coney and work in his shop for a term of ten years.

Some apprentices rebelled against the long hours of hard labor, but not Apollos. After his apprenticeship with Mr. Coney was over, he worked on his own for other goldsmiths and silversmiths. By the time he was twenty-seven, he had set aside enough money to think of marrying. His bride was Deborah Hitchbourn, the daughter of a prosperous Boston businessman.

A year or so later, Apollos opened his own shop and took out an ad for it in a newspaper. But the ad didn't use the name Apollos Rivoire; instead, it listed him as

"Paul Revere, Goldsmith & Silversmith." Some time before, like many other new-comers to America, he had changed his name to make it easier for his English-speaking friends to pronounce. And so, when his first son was born late in 1734, he was given his father's new name, and was christened Paul Revere, not Apollos Rivoire.

Young Paul was a sturdy, brown-eyed boy who had inherited the dark complexion of his French ancestors. He grew up in a crowded house on Fish Street in Boston's North End with his six brothers and sisters.

When it came time to send Paul to school, his father had two choices. Paul

A colonial boy recites his lessons in a classroom much like those in the North Writing School that the young Paul Revere attended.

Now the Child being entred in his Letters and Spelling, let him learn these and such like Sentences by Heart, whereby he will be both instructed in his Duty, and encouraged in his Learning.

The Dutiful Child's Promises,

I Will fear GOD, and honour the KING.
I will honour my Father & Mother.
I will Obey my Superiours.
I will Submit to my Elders.
I will Love my Friends.
I will hate no Man.
I will forgive my Enemies, and pray to God for them.
I will as much as in me lies keen all God's Holy Commandments.

Page from a 1727 New England primer similar to those Paul might have studied.

could go to a Latin, or grammar, school which prepared its students for Harvard and other colleges. Or, like most sons of craftsmen, he could go to a writing school which would teach him the basic skills needed in business.

Mr. Revere chose the second type, and enrolled six-year-old Paul in the North Writing School on Love Lane. There he attended reading classes on the first floor and writing classes on the second, and was quick to learn his lessons. His fellow students were all boys. In Paul's day, few girls went to school, and many women signed their names with just an "x."

Paul's formal education ended when he was twelve. That was the age when most boys left school and became apprentices to master craftsmen. In Paul's case, that meant joining his father in his workshop and learning how to be a silversmith.

First, Mr. Revere taught Paul how to heat a block of silver in a special furnace called a crucible. At about 2,000 degrees Fahrenheit, the silver melted. Paul and his father poured the liquid silver into a mold to form an ingot, or metal bar, with which they could work. Using hammers and an anvil, they flattened the ingot to the desired thickness. Then they began to pound the piece of silver into the shape of the object they were making — a spoon, a bowl, a teapot. If the metal became brittle from the pounding, they reheated it to keep it from breaking.

After more hammering and more reheat-

Silversmiths hard at work in a French workshop in the 1700s. At left, a smith pours molten silver or gold into a mold to form an ingot. In the middle, two other smiths pound an ingot flat so that it can be worked. At the right, one smith hammers a flat piece of silver into a plate, and two others shape different silver objects. While the workshop shown here is probably larger than the one in which Paul Revere learned his craft, the stages in the silversmithing process are the same.

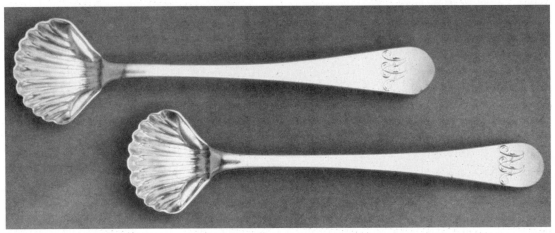

A silver teapot and tankard, and a pair of silver salt spoons, all designed and made in Paul Revere's shop.

ing, the object gradually assumed its final form. Now it was time for Paul and his father to apply the finishing touches. Using a sharp tool called a burin, they decorated the surface of the object with various designs. If it was a teapot or a pitcher, they made a handle separately and added it on with a metallic adhesive called solder. Then they polished the object with cloths to bring out its natural brilliance.

As the years passed, Mr. Revere gave Paul more difficult assignments. The boy learned quickly, and in time he became as fine a silversmith as his father. But he didn't devote all of his energies to the workshop.

The Revere family were regular church-

Early twentieth-century illustration of the young Paul Revere as a silversmith.

goers, and when he was sixteen Paul thought of a way he could serve the church and make a little money besides. With five other boys, he formed a bell ringers' society. Then Paul went to Christ Church, also known as the Old North Church, and told the rector his idea. He and his friends would ring the church's eight bells "any Time the Wardens of the Church shall desire it" in return for the modest sum of three shillings a week.

Paul must have been a convincing salesman for the rector said yes to his proposal.

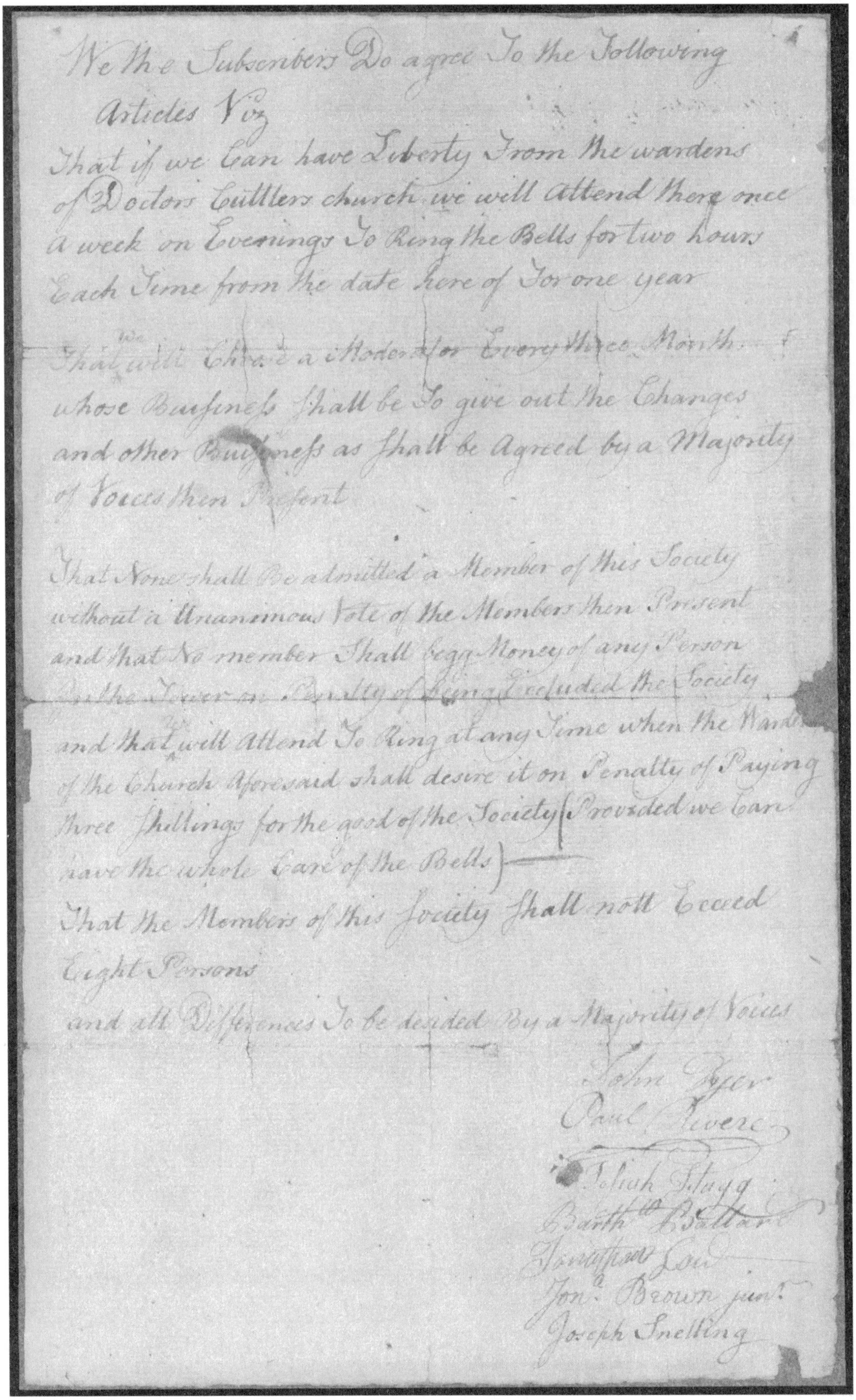

We the Subscribers Do agree To the following
Articles Viz
That if we Can have Liberty from the wardens
of Doctors Cuttlers church we will Attend there once
A week on Evenings To Ring the Bells for two hours
Each Time from the date here of for one year

That we will Chuse a Moderator Every three Month.
whose Business shall be To give out the Changes
and other Business as shall be Agreed by a Majority
of Voices then Present

That None shall Be admitted a Member of this Society
without a Unanimous Vote of the Members then Present
and that No member shall begg Money of any Person
in the Tower on Penalty of Being Excluded the Society.
and that we will Attend To Ring at any Time when the Wardens
of the Church Aforesaid shall desire it on Penalty of Paying
three Shillings for the good of the Society (Provided we Can
have the whole Care of the Bells)——

That the Members of this Society shall nott Exceed
Eight Persons
and all Differences To be decided By a Majority of Voices

John Dyer
Paul Revere

Josiah Flagg
Barth Ballard
Jonathan Law
Jon. Brown jun.
Joseph Snelling

Bell ringers' agreement, circa 1750, that Paul and six other boys wrote and signed.

To confirm the deal, Paul drew up a contract outlining the tasks he and the other boys would perform. This contract, which has been preserved, reveals several things about the young Revere. Even in his teens, he knew how to make an effective business presentation. And he was a surprisingly good writer — and speller.

When Paul was just nineteen, in 1754, his father died suddenly. Mr. Revere "left no will and no estate," his son later wrote, but he did leave "a good name, and seven children."

The law said that no person under twenty-one could run a shop, so Mrs. Revere took over her late husband's business. Paul and his younger brother Thomas did the actual work, but in the spring of 1756 Paul abruptly left and joined the Massachusetts militia as a second lieutenant. No one knows why exactly. Perhaps he had a longing for adventure. Or perhaps he just wanted to see a little of the world beyond Boston.

The Massachusetts militia reported to the British army, since America at the time was still a part of the British Empire. By the 1700s, the Empire's holdings in America consisted of thirteen colonies strung out along the East coast of today's United States. From North to South, the colonies were New Hampshire, Massachusetts, Rhode Island, Connecticut, New York, New Jersey, Pennsylvania, Delaware, Maryland, Virginia, North Carolina, South Carolina, and Georgia.

When Paul served in the Massachusetts militia alongside the British, the Empire was in the midst of a war with France — the so-called French and Indian War. At stake was the future of North America. Both Britain and France (which had established settlements in the eastern part of Canada and in Louisiana) wanted to control the land and its riches.

The Indians, who had lived in North America for centuries and are now called Native Americans, were caught between the two mighty European powers. Many tribes allied themselves with the French, with whom they had an active fur trade. Others, like the Iroquois, sided with the British.

Paul's regiment marched west to Albany, New York, then north to Fort William Henry on the shore of Lake George. And there it stayed throughout the summer and fall of 1756. The British sent out scouting parties, as did the French, but neither side felt strong enough to take the offensive.

In November, with food supplies short and winter snows coming, Paul's regiment got new orders — to return home to Massachusetts. Paul would be involved in future battles, but never again would he fight on the side of the British.

2

LIBERTY, PROPERTY, AND NO STAMPS

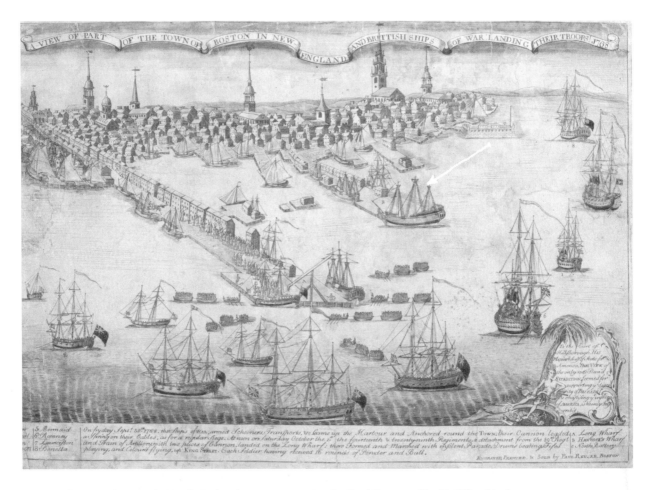

This 1768 view of Boston's North End is from an engraving by Paul Revere. Clark's Wharf is the second largest wharf in the picture. (See arrow.)

BACK IN BOSTON, PAUL SETTLED DOWN. HE TOOK OVER the management of the shop from his mother and looked for a wife. He found her in a young woman named Sara Orne, whom he called "Sary." They were married in August 1757 and moved into Paul's boyhood home near Clark's Wharf. Just nine months later their first child, a daughter, was born. They named her Deborah after Paul's mother, who lived with them.

Life was good for the Reveres in the years that followed. Paul's reputation as a master craftsman grew. Soon he had a hard time keeping up with all the orders for silver spoons, platters, and bowls that came his way. And every two years, regular as clockwork people said, his wife Sara gave birth to a new baby. But Paul's world

Large families like Paul Revere's were common in colonial America. This painting by Edward Savage (1761–1817) depicts his own family from the oldest to the youngest.

The Green Dragon Tavern, shown in the center of this drawing, was another place where Paul Revere and his friends often met to discuss the pressing issues of the day. This drawing was adapted from a watercolor by John Johnson, 1773.

wasn't limited to the shop and his family.

A sociable man, he enjoyed getting out in the evenings and exchanging ideas and opinions with his male friends. In 1760, he joined the St. Andrew's Lodge of the Masonic Fraternity, a secret society with a long history. Some said the fraternity originated in Biblical times, others that it was founded by the stonemasons who built the great cathedrals of the Middle Ages.

Freemasonry, as it was known, had spread from England to colonial America in the early 1700s and quickly became popular.

The fraternity's emphasis on charity toward the poor, and its support for religious freedom and the liberty of the individual, appealed to a wide variety of colonial Americans. Active Masons included such well-known figures as Benjamin Franklin, John Paul Jones, and George Washington.

Paul was also invited to join the Long Room Club, a discussion group that met above a printing shop in one of Boston's narrow alleys. There Paul got to know some of the city's leading thinkers. Among them were John Hancock, the wealthy heir to his

Oil painting of Dr. Joseph Warren by the famed American artist John Singleton Copley (1738–1815).

uncle Thomas's fortune, and Samuel Adams, who wrote political articles for Boston newspapers.

Another member was Dr. Joseph Warren, a fellow Mason, who became one of Paul's closest friends. As blond as Paul was dark, Dr. Warren had an outgoing personality that endeared him to his patients. He observed absolute cleanliness in his medical practice, which many doctors of the time did not. And he was an eloquent speaker.

Most of the members of the Long Room Club were graduates of Harvard College, whereas Paul had only finished the North Writing School. But his fellow members did not look down on Paul because he had not gone to college. Instead, they appreciated his skill as a craftsman, his clear thinking, and his willingness to work hard at whatever task he was assigned.

The seven-year-long French and Indian War finally ended in 1763. The British won, but the price was high: thousands of casualties and masses of debt. To help pay off their war debts, the British Parliament decided to levy new taxes on the American colonies. The colonies had benefited from the defeat of Britain's foes, the French and their Indian allies. Why shouldn't they help pay the costs of the war?

Americans, like Paul and the other members of the Long Room Club, didn't see it that way. Resentment over British trade practices had been building for a long time in Boston and other places. The British insisted that colonies sell them raw materials like lumber and cotton at low prices. Then they forced the colonists to buy manufactured goods like tools and machinery from Britain at high prices. And all the colonists' purchases had to be paid in British currency, the pound.

Bostonians reading the Stamp Act.

Protest against the Stamp Act in the streets of Boston, 1765.

Now Parliament wanted to burden the colonists with additional taxes. To make matters worse, the colonies had no representatives in Parliament to argue their case. A cry of protest went up from one of Paul's fellow Masons, James Otis: "Taxation without representation is tyranny!"

The conflict came to a head in 1765. Ignoring the protests of Otis and others, Parliament passed the Stamp Act. When it took effect, Americans would have to buy a special English stamp to put on all legal documents and official papers, and even their daily newspaper.

Colonial reaction was swift and strong. In Boston, Samual Adams had founded a new organization, the Sons of Liberty, and Paul Revere designed a special emblem for its members to wear. When word came that Parliament had passed the Stamp Act, Adams, Revere, and other Sons of Liberty led a procession to the State House. There they marched past the council chamber where the Royal Governor, Sir Francis Bernard, was holding a meeting. Council members rushed to the windows to see what was going on, and heard the marchers chanting: "Liberty, Property, and No Stamps!"

The protests must have had an effect on Parliament, for in the spring of 1766 word reached Boston that the Stamp Act had been repealed. In response, the city planned a grand celebration. All the homes in Boston were lighted with candles, fireworks blazed across the sky, and a giant, oiled paper lantern was illuminated on Boston Common. It's likely that Paul Revere had a hand in the design of the lantern and the symbols painted on it.

Besides protesting the Stamp Act, some Bostonians adopted harsher measures. If they spotted a British agent trying to collect the hated tax, they seized the man, stripped off his clothes, spread him with tar, and covered him with goose feathers. Then they paraded him through the streets before finally letting him go.

The silver Liberty Bowl, considered one of Paul Revere's finest works.

As things turned out, Boston celebrated too soon. In 1767, Parliament proclaimed that Britain still had the right to tax the American colonies whenever it felt like it. A year later, Parliament made good on its proclamation by levying new taxes on glass, paper, paint, and tea. Once again, an angry cry went up: "No taxation without representation!"

In Boston, the Sons of Liberty urged residents not to buy British manufactured goods. The members of the Massachusetts General Court, who were elected by the people, not appointed by the British, went further. They voted to send a letter to all the other colonies, warning them of what might happen if the new taxes were allowed to go into effect. What would stop the British from taxing farm products from New England, lumber from Georgia, or tobacco from Virginia?

When Parliament heard of the Court's letter, it was furious and the King himself demanded that the members retract what they had written. A poll was taken, and 92 of the Court's 109 members voted "No."

To honor the Court's refusal, the Sons of Liberty commissioned Paul Revere to make a large and handsome punchbowl. On its glistening silver surface he engraved an inscription praising the 92 men who had voted to stand by what they had said in the letter. The bowl is considered one of Revere's finest works, and is known today as the "Liberty Bowl."

3

"THE HORRID MASSACRE IN KING STREET"

PAUL WASN'T GETTING MANY OTHER ORDERS FOR HIS SILVER, however. Boston had sunk into an economic slump because of the tensions with Great Britain, and there was little demand for silver spoons and pitchers.

To fill the gap in his income, Paul decided to learn some new skills. He taught himself how to make copper engravings from which cartoons and illustrations could be printed. And he studied dentistry.

In September 1768, Paul ran an ad in the *Boston Gazette*: "This is to inform all persons who are so unfortunate as to lose their Teeth by accident that they may have them replaced by artificial ones, that look as well as Natural, by PAUL REVERE Goldsmith, near the Head of Dr. Clark's Wharf, Boston."

Meanwhile, protests against the new taxes continued in Boston. When the British sent customs officials from London to collect them, Paul and the other Sons of Liberty went into action. They blackened

Beaver.——2 Senegal.——3 Martin.——4 Glaſgow.——5 Mermaid.——6 Romney.——7 Lanceſton.——8 Bonetta.

Eight British warships arrive in Boston Harbor in 1768. Metal-cut engraving by Paul Revere.

their faces, pulled nightcaps down over their heads, and attacked any officials who dared to walk the streets after dark. At last the officials became so frightened that they and their families fled to the fortress on Castle Island in Boston Harbor.

The British responded quickly and forcefully to this setback. On September 30, 1768, a fleet of eight British warships, their cannons loaded, sailed into Boston Harbor. More than six hundred soldiers were aboard the ships. Their mission: to police the streets of Boston and prevent further attacks on the British and their supporters.

Paul watched the arrival of the ships, which he called an "insolent parade." It

made him so angry that he decided to record the event in an engraving. Paul was not an artist, so he traced a watercolor of the scene, painted by a friend. Then he transferred the tracing to a copper plate to create his engraving.

In Paul's day, there were no photographs, and newspapers ran few if any woodcut illustrations. If people wanted to see a picture of a news event, they had to buy an engraving. Hundreds of copies of Paul's engraving of the ships were printed, and they sold quickly.

Some time earlier, Parliament had passed a "Quartering Act" that required the colonies to provide housing for British soldiers stationed in their towns and cities. But the Sons of Liberty urged Bostonians not to co-operate when the British troops landed. Citizen after citizen refused to take the soldiers in, and they had to stay in tents or in public buildings and warehouses.

Over the next eighteen months, small boys often threw rocks at the British soldiers, and the soldiers in turn chased the boys and roughed them up. But there were no serious clashes between soldiers and civilians in Boston. Not, that is, until the night of March 5, 1770.

It all began when a wigmaker accused a British officer of not paying for a repair to his wig. The wigmaker ordered his young apprentice to follow the officer and get the money from him. The officer tried to escape to King Street, where a British guardhouse was located. The apprentice followed, shouting that the officer was a thief, and soon a crowd had gathered.

A British sentry was stationed on King Street near the guardhouse. When the apprentice continued to taunt the officer, the sentry intervened and struck the youth. The apprentice screamed in pain, the angry crowd surged forward, and the officer called for help from the guards.

Seven armed British guards, led by Captain John Preston, emerged from the guardhouse in response to the officer's call. They confronted the crowd, at the front of

which stood a tall and muscular African-American sailor, Crispus Attucks. Captain Preston urged the crowd to disperse and go home, but instead the townspeople lunged toward the sentry and the guards.

Blows were exchanged, someone shouted "Fire!", and shots rang out. A moment later four bodies lay dead in the snow. Crispus Attucks was the first to fall.

Was Paul Revere on the scene? There's no record of it, but later he sketched an exact diagram of King Street, showing the positions of each of the dead. This suggests he *was* present on the fateful night. Later, he cut an engraving that pictured a line of British guards firing into the crowd. The engraving was hand-colored to highlight the red of the guards' uniforms — and the blood of the fallen.

Thousands of copies of the engraving, titled "a Representation of the late horrid Massacre in King St.," were distributed throughout the colonies. Before the incident, many Americans had been angry with their British rulers; now they became downright furious.

Both sides attempted to calm down the situation. In the weeks that followed the Boston Massacre, the British transferred most of their troops quartered in the city to Castle Island. The Boston courts gave the British officers and soldiers involved in the massacre a fair trial, and acquitted all

Paul Revere's engraving of the Boston Massacre.

but two. And Parliament abolished most of the hated taxes. Only one was left in place — a modest tax on tea that no one thought the colonists would object to.

Paul Revere's business must have been doing well in 1770, for he bought his first house that year. Earlier he had always rented. Built about 1680, his new home was located on North Square and had three stories. Even so, it must have been crowded, for it housed not only Paul, his wife, and their children, but also Paul's widowed mother. Mrs. Revere insisted on paying her son room and board, which was the custom in those days when parents lived with their grown children.

Paul Revere's new home on North Square as it looks now.

In back of the house was a yard on which Paul built a barn for his horse, a reddish-brown mare. Paul did not need the horse to get to work since his shop was close to his home. He must have ridden the mare for pleasure. In the open country beyond the city limits, she could cover a mile in less than three minutes.

Tragedy struck the Revere household in 1773. A few months after giving birth to her eighth child, Paul's wife Sara died in May at the age of thirty-six. Paul's mother took over the care of the sickly baby, a girl named Isanna, as well as the other Revere children.

Paul's reactions to his wife's death were not recorded. No doubt he grieved for Sara,

his loyal companion of almost sixteen years. But he knew his children needed a step-mother to look after them. And he himself needed a partner to help him in his busy life.

Sometime that summer Paul met a forth-right young woman named Rachel Walker. She liked Paul, and he liked her. She also made a good impression on his children, and his mother, and helped the family to get over the loss of little Isanna, who died in September. Later that month Rachel and Paul were married, and she moved into her husband's home on North Square.

Meanwhile, the conflict between the Sons of Liberty and their British overlords had died down after the Boston Massacre.

Portrait of Rachel Walker, Paul Revere's second wife. Paul commissioned this miniature, which was painted on ivory by Joseph Dunkerly and is just 1½" high, half the size of this picture. Sometimes miniatures were painted with brushes containing a single hair! This portrait is set in a gold frame that Paul probably made himself.

But it flared up anew in the late fall of 1773. The huge East India Company was on the verge of bankruptcy. To help save it, Parliament passed the Tea Act that gave the Company a monopoly on the American market. Even worse, Parliament appointed special agents to sell the Company's tea in the colonies and pocket the profits. American merchants were completely cut out.

A great hue and cry arose throughout the colonies. If the British could enforce a monopoly on the sale of tea, what would be next? Cloth, shoes, wine? The protest was loudest in Boston. There the Sons of Liberty demanded that the Company's agents resign from their jobs. When they refused, the Sons threatened stronger action.

*T*HE BOSTON TEA PARTY

*S*HIPS FILLED WITH CARGOES OF TEA WERE ALREADY SAILING toward American ports. The first to arrive in Boston was the *Dartmouth*. The Sons warned its owner not to unload the vessel "on his peril." Twenty-five members of the Sons, armed with muskets and bayonets, stood guard that night to make sure the owner obeyed the warning. Among them was Paul Revere.

The next day, the Sons decided that nearby seaports should be alerted that British tea ships might try to unload at their docks. In a time before the telegraph and telephone had been invented, the only means of speedy communication was a rider on a fast horse. So the Sons assigned five horsemen, including Paul, to carry their urgent message.

Paul must have been an excellent rider for this would be only the first of many rides he would make on behalf of the Revolution. We don't know where he was headed on that December day, or how long it took him to ride there and back. But he must have had to fight weariness all the way, since he'd had no sleep the night before.

In Boston, meanwhile, two more tea-

Bostonians line up on Griffin's Wharf to cheer the destruction of the tea.

ships joined the *Dartmouth* at Griffin's Wharf. A huge crowd in Old South Meeting House agreed with Samuel Adams that all three ships must return to England without unloading. But the royal governor wouldn't let them leave the wharf.

Samuel Adams announced the governor's decision to the crowd at Old South, saying, "This meeting can do nothing more to save the country." In response, a man jumped up, shouting "To Griffin's Wharf!" Another yelled, "Boston Harbor will be a teapot tonight!"

That night more than a hundred men, most of them Sons of Liberty, gathered at the wharf where the three tea ships were docked. The men wore ragged clothes and had darkened their faces with soot or lamp black so they would not be recognized. As part of their disguise, many of the men carried tomahawks like those used by Native Americans.

Hundreds of other Bostonians watched from the wharf as the men boarded the first of the ships. After getting the key to the hold, the men hauled the tea chests up onto the deck, broke them open, and hurled them into the water. Once all the tea from the first ship had been disposed of, the men moved on to the other ships and repeated the process. No one tried to stop them. By the time the men had finished, Boston Harbor was awash with tea.

Was Paul one of those who dumped the tea? Legend says he was, and his name appears (along with that of his friend, Dr. Joseph Warren) in a song about the event that was written immediately afterward by an unknown poet.

Rally Mohawks! Bring out your axes,
And tell King George we'll pay no taxes
On his foreign tea . . .
Our Warren's here and bold Revere
With hands to do and words to cheer
For Liberty and laws . . .

Sons of Liberty board a tea ship in Boston Harbor, haul up the tea chests from the hold, and get ready to dump them in the harbor.

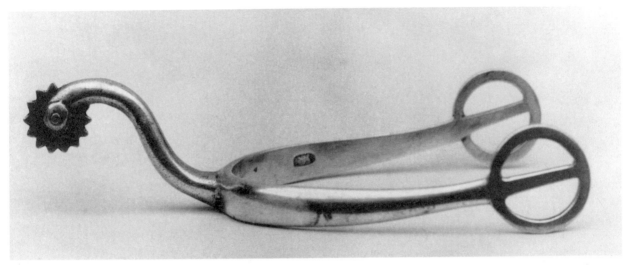

Many museums display spurs that Paul Revere supposedly used. This spur may actually have been worn by Paul. It's made of silver and bears his mark.

What we do know for sure is that the day after the Boston Tea Party, as it came to be known, Paul Revere set out once again. This time he rode to New York and then on to Philadelphia to tell sympathizers in those cities what had happened in Boston.

Starting out before dawn on a hired horse, Paul followed a route mail riders — the mailmen of their day — had carved out over the years. The route headed west from Boston to Worcester and Springfield, Massachusetts, then turned south to Hartford and New Haven, Connecticut, and southwest from there to New York City. The dirt roads Paul traveled were dusty in dry weather, muddy when wet, and always rough.

After meeting with fellow rebels in New York, Paul climbed back into the saddle and took a ferry across the Hudson River to New Jersey. Picking up speed, he rode south through New Jersey to Trenton, where he boarded another ferry that carried him and his horse across the Delaware River to Pennsylvania. From there it wasn't far to his final destination, Philadelphia.

Along the way, Paul was glad to find taverns in many of the towns and villages through which he rode. At them he could obtain food and drink for himself, and his horse could be rubbed down, watered, and replaced if necessary. If it was late in the day, Paul could rent a room for the night.

But there was no guarantee he would sleep well. It was common practice at the

Paul Revere's leather saddlebags.

time for two or more strangers of the same gender to share a single bed. And bedbugs were a constant threat to a person's rest.

However he had slept, Paul would be back in the saddle before dawn the next morning, ready to ride on to his next stop. On this trip, which was about 350 miles each way, he averaged more than 60 miles a day. He rode into Boston just eleven days after he had left.

Back in his shop, Paul caught up on a pileup of orders for silver. But it wasn't long before he was involved again in the ongoing conflict with Great Britain.

Parliament hadn't forgotten the Tea Party. In the spring of 1774, it sent General Thomas Gage to take command of the Massachusetts colony, and to punish Boston. The city's port, upon which Boston depended, was to be closed to all seaborne traffic until the city agreed to pay for the tea that had been destroyed. If the Bostonians refused, the British were prepared to starve them into submission.

Once again, the Sons of Liberty called upon Paul to make the long and difficult ride to New York and Philadelphia. His mission: to win support for Boston in its time of need.

His message was greeted more warmly than he had expected. New Yorkers expressed their firm determination to stand by Boston, and Philadelphians went even further. They made plans for a Continental Congress that would discuss the colonies' strained relations with Great Britain and what to do about them.

When Paul returned to Boston, General Gage, the new British overlord, was busy closing down the port. Soon, 5,000 British soldiers arrived to occupy the city. Boston at the time had a population of around 15,000, which meant there was one soldier for every three citizens. The soldiers camped out on Boston Common.

In the weeks that followed, neighboring towns and cities supplied Boston with essential food supplies. So did the other colonies: South Carolina sent rice, Maryland cornmeal and flour. But times were still hard.

Not everyone disagreed with General Gage's harsh measures. Those loyal to the British — and there were many — hoped his strict rules would bring peace and order to Boston. Hundreds of Tories, as the British supporters were called, crowded into the city for protection.

Meanwhile, General Gage cracked down further on his opponents. He forbade most of the town meetings by which New Englanders had always governed themselves. Rebel leaders like Samuel and John Adams could now be sent to England for trial. If charged and convicted of treason, they faced death by hanging.

Rebels called these latest rules the "Intolerable Acts." Dr. Joseph Warren organized a meeting in Suffolk County near Boston to protest them. The meeting issued a set of resolutions known as the "Suffolk Resolves." They proclaimed the Intolerable Acts unconstitutional. But

Portrait of General Thomas Gage by John Singleton Copley. Gage commanded the British troops that occupied Boston.

that was just the start: the Resolves also urged the people of Massachusetts to form their own government, and get ready to defend it by force if necessary.

The First Continental Congress was in session in Philadelphia and needed to be informed of the Resolves at once. Paul Revere agreed to take on the assignment — his most important ride thus far.

MESSENGER
FOR THE
REVOLUTION

PAUL LEFT BOSTON on September 11, 1774, and reached Philadelphia just five days later, breaking his own record for speed.

The next day the Congress members voted overwhelmingly to endorse the Resolves. Until then, many of the delegates had hoped a compromise could be worked out with Great Britain. But now, by endorsing the use of force against British troops if necessary, they helped to pave the way for armed resistance.

Paul returned to Boston with his good news on September 23. However, he had only a few days to rest and work in his shop. On September 29 he was on the road once more, this time to inform supporters in New York and Philadelphia of the latest developments in Massachusetts.

Rebel leaders like Samuel Adams, John Hancock, and Joseph Warren may have been better known to the general public. But Paul Revere had earned his own claim to fame. He became known as "The Messenger for the Revolution" — a man you could always count on to get things done.

On December 7, 1774, Rachel Revere gave birth to her first child, a son whom she

A session of the First Continental Congress. Patrick Henry of Virginia, who famously said "Give me liberty, or give me death," is the speaker.

and Paul named Joshua. But his father had little time to spend with the new baby. The Sons of Liberty wanted him to ride again, this time to Portsmouth, New Hampshire, sixty miles north of Boston.

The Sons had learned that General Gage planned to dispatch several regiments by sea to Portsmouth to reinforce Fort William and Mary. The fort contained a large store of guns and ammunition, and the General had gotten word that local rebels were planning to seize them.

Paul saddled his horse and set out early in the morning of December 13. The rutted roads were icy, and a stiff wind was blowing, but Paul still managed to reach Portsmouth by late afternoon. He alerted the leader of the town's militia that the British were on the way, and the man took action at once.

Overnight the leader rounded up 400 volunteers. At noon the next day, under cover of a snowstorm, the militiamen surrounded the fort and demanded its surrender. Although they were badly

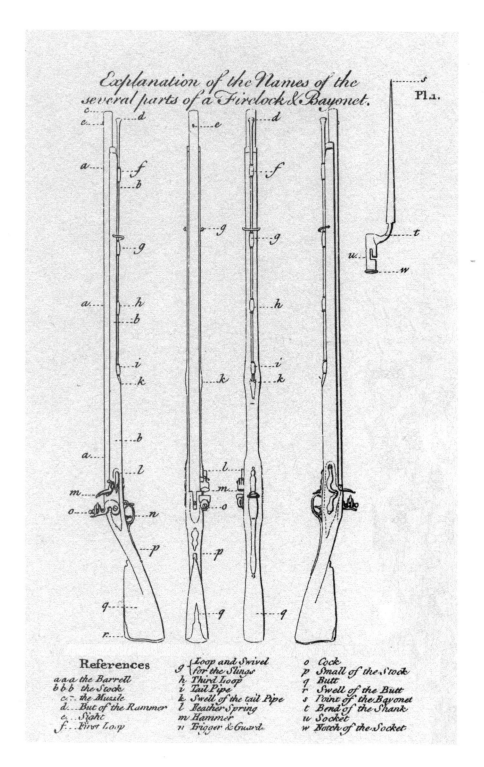

The Long Land Pattern musket diagrammed above was made in London in 1759. It was used during the American Revolution by both British soldiers and American militiamen.

outnumbered, the six British soldiers guarding the fort fought bravely until they were overpowered.

The victorious militiamen rushed inside, broke down the door to the storeroom, and hauled out more than 100 barrels of gunpowder. Many muskets and 16 cannons were also carried away. The militiamen hid the arms and powder at various places in and around Portsmouth. They would come in handy if open warfare ever broke out between America and Great Britain.

Paul did not take part in the attack on the fort. Instead he — and his horse — rested in preparation for the long, hard ride back to Boston the next day. He reached home safely long before the British reinforcements arrived by ship in Portsmouth.

General Gage was furious when he learned what had happened in New Hampshire. He knew Paul Revere was the one who had alerted the Portsmouth militia, but hesitated to arrest him. The General worried that such an action would only lead to more unrest. Instead, he ordered that Revere's movements be watched, and he put in place strict new travel restrictions. From now on, anyone entering or leaving Boston would have to show a pass.

Boston was tense that winter of 1774–75. The British were suspicious of the city's residents, and they, in turn, were wary of the British. Paul and other Sons of Liberty patrolled the city streets secretly at night, keeping a close eye on what the British soldiers were up to.

In the spring, General Gage planned a major military action. One of his spies reported that the rebels had amassed arms in Concord, a small town just twenty miles west of Boston. Fearing the arms would be used against his men, Gage decided they must be seized.

Paul Revere and his fellow Sons of Liberty had their spies, too. The spies informed them of Gage's plan, and Paul was assigned to alert the Concord militia. He managed to get out of Boston and rode swiftly to Concord where he told militia leaders of the British scheme. The militiamen quickly removed the threatened arms from a warehouse where they had been stored. They hid the guns and ammunition in various safe places around Concord.

Meanwhile, back in Boston, General Gage told his best soldiers to be prepared for fresh orders. The Sons of Liberty took this to mean the British would soon be on the move. Once again Paul, carrying a forged pass, dared to ride out of the city, this time to warn Samuel Adams and John Hancock that the British were coming

Samuel Adams, portrait by John Singleton Copley.

Portrait of John Hancock, also painted by John Singleton Copley.

and might arrest them. The rebel leaders had left Boston and were staying with friends in Lexington, a town halfway between Boston and Concord.

Paul completed the second ride successfully, but General Gage took steps to ensure he wouldn't make another. The general posted guards at checkpoints along all the roads from Boston to Concord. Their mission: to keep watch day and night and check the identity of anyone who tried to get past them.

6

CAPTURED

ON APRIL 18, PAUL'S GOOD FRIEND DR. JOSEPH WARREN GOT word that the British would make their move that night at midnight. The soldiers — between 800 and 900 of them — would be rowed across Back Bay from Boston to Cambridge. From there they would march to Concord.

Dr. Warren summoned Paul to his house at once. He told Revere he should get ready to alert the militia in Lexington and Concord that the British were coming that night. But this time Paul would not ride alone. The doctor thought two horsemen would have a better chance of eluding the British guards than just one. William Dawes, another loyal Son of Liberty, had agreed to take the single land route out of Boston. At the same time, Paul would row across Boston Harbor to Charlestown, pick up a borrowed horse there, and ride on to Lexington and Concord via a different route.

The Old North Church had the tallest steeple in Boston. Earlier that week, Paul had arranged with Old North's sexton to send a signal as soon as the British travel

plans were known. If the British troops left Boston by land, the sexton was to hang one lighted lantern in the steeple. But if the troops left by water, the sexton was to hang two. The signals from the lanterns could easily be seen across the river in Charlestown.

After his meeting with Dr. Warren, Paul walked quickly to the Old North Church to find the sexton. He told him that the British would definitely be going by water, and the sexton summoned a trusted church worker to help him. The two men immediately began the long climb to the top of the steeple. There, as planned, they hung two lighted lanterns from the highest window.

Meanwhile, Paul hastened to his home, and his wife helped him pull on his heavy riding boots. Then he strode through dark streets to the waterfront where his small boat was docked. Two experienced boatmen were waiting for him. The three men pushed off and rowed across the harbor toward the Charlestown ferry landing. But a British warship, the *Somerset*, loomed in their path. It had been stationed there in midriver to prevent messengers like Paul from leaving Boston.

Fortunately the moon was low on the horizon. Paul and the boatmen were able

Illustration of the Old North Church with two lanterns lit in its steeple.

Paul and the two boatmen spot the British warship Somerset *as they start to row across the harbor toward Charlestown. Painting by the twentieth-century artist A. Lassell Ripley.*

to make their way past the warship without being noticed. They reached Charlestown safely, and Paul was led to his borrowed horse, a spirited mare named Brown Beauty. Paul sprang into the saddle and set off toward Lexington.

He hadn't gone far when he spotted two British guards waiting by the side of the road ahead. Paul quickly swung his horse around and sped back the way he had come. The two guards saw him and gave chase, but Brown Beauty was too fast for them. Paul turned into a side road and made a

long detour that finally brought him to Lexington.

He had just warned Samuel Adams and John Hancock that the British were on the way when the other rider, William Dawes, arrived. Luckily Dawes had known the sergeant of the guard at the Boston checkpoint, and the man had passed him through without question.

Revere and Dawes didn't stay long in Lexington. They guessed that the main British force must be close behind them by now, and the Concord militia still had to be warned. This time Paul and Dawes rode together, and they were soon joined by Samuel Prescott, a young doctor who was returning to his home in Concord.

Paul alerted the others to be on the lookout for British guards along the road, and sure enough he soon glimpsed two in the shadows ahead. He and his companions decided to ride on and fight the guards if

necessary. But as they spurred their horses forward, two more guards emerged from the trees and lined up with their fellows.

Revere, Dawes, and Prescott tried to break through the line, but they were outnumbered. The British commanded them to halt and herded the trio into a nearby pasture. However, the Americans weren't ready to accept defeat. At a signal from

Portrait of William Dawes, Paul Revere's fellow rider on the midnight ride. This painting is attributed to John Johnson (1753–1818).

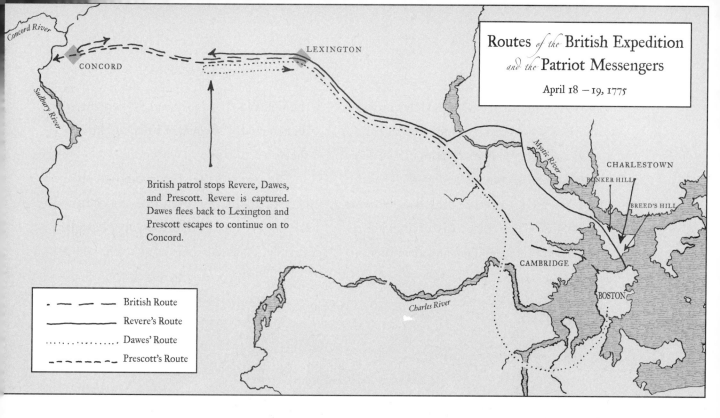

CONCORD

LEXINGTON

CHARLESTOWN

BUNKER HILL

BREED'S HILL

CAMBRIDGE

BOSTON

Mystic River

Charles River

Concord River

Sudbury River

British patrol stops Revere, Dawes, and Prescott. Revere is captured. Dawes flees back to Lexington and Prescott escapes to continue on to Concord.

- ·— — — British Route
- ———— Revere's Route
- ············ Dawes' Route
- – – – – – Prescott's Route

Dr. Prescott, they split apart. Dr. Prescott urged his horse to the left while Paul rode to the right and Dawes turned back to the road they had just left.

Dawes thought he was in the clear, but before he had gone very far his horse was frightened by something in the road. The animal threw him off and raced away, leaving Dawes lying in the mud. When he caught his breath, he stumbled back toward Lexington.

It was a different story for Dr. Prescott. He made his way through woods and swamps and succeeded in eluding the British guards. Prescott galloped into Concord an hour or so later and accomplished what Paul had meant to do: He alerted the militia that the British soldiers were on the march.

From Concord, the word went out to nearby towns, and soon all the militias in the vicinity were mobilizing.

As for Paul, he had intended to escape into the woods, when six more British guards suddenly appeared in front of him. The guards were leading several Americans they had captured on the road that night. The party was joined by the other four guards who had failed to stop Prescott and Dawes. Paul was ordered to dismount, and a British officer in the group started to question him.

But Paul turned the tables on the officer. He told the man how he had alerted the countryside all the way from Boston to Lexington. And he predicted that the large British force marching toward Lexington and Concord would be attacked by hordes of militiamen who had responded to his call.

Alarmed by Paul's prediction, the officer ordered him to mount his horse. Then he and his men escorted Paul back toward Lexington. Their plan was to join forces with their fellow soldiers and alert them to the dangers that lay ahead. When the soldiers neared the town, a volley of gunshots shattered the quiet.

Paul guessed the shots were part of the general alarm. However, the officer feared the shots signaled that the Americans had already launched their attack. He and his

Paul tries to elude the British guards who are determined to capture him.

men would have to move more quickly if the advancing British troops were to be warned in time.

To travel faster, the officer decided he must free Paul and the other prisoners. But the British took Brown Beauty for one of their own men to ride. It was the last Paul saw of the sturdy mare.

The prisoners scattered and Paul set out on foot toward Lexington. It was now almost three A.M. He was surprised to find Samuel Adams and John Hancock still arguing in the house where he had left them two hours earlier. Hancock wanted to join the local militia and fight alongside them. Adams was trying to convince his friend that he was more valuable as a leader behind the scenes.

Paul sided with Adams, and together they finally persuaded Hancock to leave Lexington. The two men had been offered refuge in the nearby village of Woburn. After escorting them there, Paul returned to Lexington. Hancock's clerk, John Lowell, came running up to him as he approached Lexington Green.

The young man told Paul that Hancock's trunk, filled with important papers about the rebels' plans, had been left behind at the Buckman Tavern. The trunk must be removed and hidden away, he said, before the British arrived. Paul agreed, and hurried with Lowell to the tavern. They got there just as a militiaman informed the crowd in

John Hancock's trunk.

the taproom that the British were less than a mile away.

Paul and Lowell raced upstairs and found the large trunk. They managed to lug it downstairs and stumbled out the front door with it. Without pausing to rest, they started across the green where the Lexington militia was assembling to meet the British. At the same moment, the first of the redcoated British soldiers came into view at the far end of the green.

Paul remained calm in the midst of the frenzied scene. Behind him, he heard the leader of the militia shout: "Stand your ground! Don't fire unless fired upon!" But he kept his mind focused on his goal — to find a hiding place for the trunk somewhere beyond the green.

7

THE BRITISH RETREAT

A SINGLE SHOT RANG OUT, BUT PAUL COULD NOT TELL WHICH side had fired it. He and Lowell had left the green by now. As they struggled into the woods with their heavy burden, more shots were heard. They lumbered on, though, and finally found a good spot to hide Hancock's trunk.

And that's the last that was heard of Paul until he surfaced again the next day. But his warning to the militia at Lexington, a warning that spread out from there to the militias of many other towns, was responsible for much of what happened in the next twenty-four hours.

It's not clear who fired first when the British and American fighters confronted each other on Lexington Green. But the deadly result was more than clear. One British soldier was wounded, while the Americans suffered eight dead and nine wounded. The surviving militiamen vowed the outcome would be different the next time they met the British.

From Lexington, the British marched on to their actual destination, Concord. Their

The battle on Lexington Green, as engraved by A. Doolittle in 1775.

assignment was to find and destroy the rebels' hidden cache of arms and ammunition. After what had happened in Lexington, the British commanders knew it wouldn't be easy. But they didn't expect the reception that awaited them.

When the British reached Concord, they were surprised to find no militiamen in the town center. Nor did they find any arms in the inn and other buildings where their spies had told them the weapons were stored. The townspeople had moved them to safer places following Paul Revere's visit three days earlier.

While the British were searching the town and the farms to the north of it, the Concord militia had been busy. They had sent word to the militias of nearby towns, and now more than 500 armed men were gathered in a field outside Concord. Colo-

American militiamen and British soldiers clash at the North Bridge in Concord, April 19, 1775.

nel James Barrett, the militia leader, order-ed his men to load their weapons. Then he gave the order to advance.

The British were startled when they saw the large American force approaching the North Bridge over the Concord River. Shots were exchanged, and there were casualties on both sides. But most of the fighters remained in place, neither advanc-ing nor retreating. Only when more and more militias arrived to join the rebel forces did the British fall back to the center of Concord.

They didn't stop there. With the militia-men in pursuit, the British retreated toward Boston. The militiamen had a clear advantage. They knew the countryside and could fire at the British from behind the stone fences that lined both sides of the narrow road. Mile by mile, the British casualties mounted.

By the time they reached Lexington, the British were in full retreat. At Lexington, they were cheered briefly by the arrival of reinforcements sent out by General Gage from Boston. But the rebel forces were being reinforced constantly, too. Militias from towns as far away as Salem and Marblehead joined the rebel ranks as the day progressed.

The Americans took their share of casualties, but the British suffered far more dead and wounded. They blamed the fighting tactics employed by the Americans for their losses. A British admiral, Samuel Graves, commander of the British navy in Boston, wrote to his superiors: "The Rebels followed the Indian manner of fighting, concealing themselves behind hedges, trees and skulking in the woods and houses, whereby usually they galled our soldiers exceedingly."

A wounded British soldier, in a letter home, echoed the admiral's words: "They did not fight us like a regular army, only like savages behind trees and stone walls. . . ."

At dusk, the retreating British finally reached Charlestown where they were protected by British warships stationed in Boston Harbor. The Americans realized they stood no chance against the ships and halted their pursuit. However, they blocked the only land approach to Charlestown, cutting off all supplies of food from the countryside.

The rebel leaders gathered in the nearby town of Cambridge to plot their next moves. Paul Revere joined them on the morning of April 20, the day after the British retreat from Concord. He had probably spent most of the day before getting some rest after his nightlong ride.

Dr. Joseph Warren and the other leaders realized that everything had changed as a result of the clashes at Lexington and Concord. Before, the colonies' conflict with Britain had been largely a battle of words. Now it had exploded into open warfare.

The rebels had two immediate tasks. The first was to get word to the colonists from New Hampshire to Georgia of what had happened at Lexington and Concord. Teams of relay riders set out at once to accomplish this goal. They carried with them a vivid account of the battles, designed to rally support for the rebel cause.

The second task was to raise an army of at least 8,000 men for an expected siege of Boston. Paul Revere agreed to take on this assignment. Riding a hired horse, he traveled from one New England town to another. At every stop he met with local committees and explained why it was

Paul rides throughout New England, spreading the word about the skirmishes at Lexington and Concord, and urging volunteers to enlist in the new American army.

urgent to enlist an army to defend their homes and families.

The men of New England, responding to the rebel leaders' call, volunteered in large numbers. But now another problem arose: How would these new soldiers be paid? The colonial monetary system was linked to Britain's. However, the British had never supplied the colonies with enough silver coins, and had prohibited the colonists from making their own.

As a substitute, the colonists used paper money, or "bills of credit," which were meant to be exchanged later for coin. Even paper money was in short supply, though. The rebel leaders, who had moved from Cambridge to nearby Watertown, remembered that Paul was a master engraver as well as a silversmith. They hired him to cut copper plates and to print enough paper money to meet their needs.

Paul moved to Watertown and went to work. He also made contact with his wife in Boston, told her where he was, and urged her to join him with the rest of the family. His oldest son and chief assistant, fifteen-year-old Paul Jr., could stay behind to watch over the shop.

Rachel Revere managed to obtain a pass for herself and the six other children and they left Boston in early May. It was a strange scene at the checkpoint. While Rachel and other rebel families were eager to get out of the city, hundreds of families loyal to Britain were flocking into Boston for protection.

Examples of colonial paper money engraved by Paul Revere.

THE
BATTLE
OF
BREED'S HILL

BACK IN WATERTOWN, THE MASSACHUSETTS REBEL LEADERS were discussing their next military move. They decided to send troops under cover of night to fortify Bunker Hill on the Charlestown peninsula. The hill would give the American forces a commanding view of Boston Harbor. It would also provide a base from which a future attack on the city could be launched.

The troops set out on the night of June 16. When they reached the peninsula they realized that Breed's Hill, which was next to Bunker Hill, would be a better site for the base. They began to dig, and by dawn the next morning they had constructed a sizable earthen fortress.

When General Gage saw what was happening, he ordered his artillerymen to fire

on the hill. Some American soldiers scrambled for cover, but most of them carried on with their work as British cannonballs landed near them.

Next, the British sent boatloads of redcoated soldiers across Boston Harbor. The soldiers came aground at the foot of Breed's Hill and prepared to climb the slope to the hastily built fortress. As they began their

American militiamen atop Breed's Hill direct their fire at the oncoming British in this twentieth-century painting.

journey upward, the British expected to be fired upon at any moment. But no Americans appeared on the hill, and not a sound came from the fortress.

The British were less than fifteen paces from the top when the air around them suddenly exploded with musket fire. The Americans in the fortress were fighting back at last. One redcoat after another fell in his tracks, and the rest stumbled down the slope to the safety of their boats.

Before the day was over, the British launched two more attacks on Breed's Hill.

Neither of them was any more successful than the first. Only when the Americans ran out of ammunition during the third attack did the redcoats manage to reach the top of the hill.

For the British, the Battle of Bunker Hill, as it mistakenly came to be called, was more of a defeat than a victory. When the redcoats got to the fortress, it was empty: The American defenders had retreated safely in the gathering dusk.

The British had also suffered far greater losses than the Americans. Of the 2,500 or so redcoats who had stormed the hill, almost half — 1,054 men — now lay dead or wounded. The Americans did not escape unscathed. They had sent 3,000 soldiers to fortify Breed's Hill, and 414 of them had been killed or wounded in the struggle. One of those who had died was Paul Revere's good friend, Dr. Joseph Warren.

Paul did not take part in the fighting. He was still busy in Watertown, making paper money for the rebel cause. Meanwhile, in Philadelphia, the Second Continental Con-

gress was in session. Samuel Adams and his cousin John reported on the bloody events at Lexington and Concord, and the Congress reacted by laying plans for the first Continental Army. The delegates asked George Washington to command it.

The foundation of the new army would be the soldiers Paul had helped to recruit a few weeks earlier. General Washington arrived in Cambridge to take charge of the untrained men and shape them into a fighting force. One of their greatest needs was

In this scene, also painted by a twentieth-century artist, British soldiers struggle to reach the top of Breed's Hill.

gunpowder, but no factory in Massachusetts knew how to make it.

General Washington and the rebel leaders had heard of Paul's many skills, from silversmithing to making false teeth. Now they called upon Revere to learn yet another — the manufacture of gunpowder.

A factory in Philadelphia was known to make the best powder in America. Paul rode to the factory, won the cooperation of the owner, and obtained the information he needed. Back in Massachusetts, he oversaw the building of a powder mill in the town of Canton. Construction of the mill began in January 1776, and by May it was producing a steady supply of gunpowder for the army.

While Paul Revere was learning how to make gunpowder, his beloved Boston was enduring a difficult winter and spring. General Gage, his reputation damaged by the Battle of Bunker Hill, had been called back to England in October. He was succeeded by General William Howe, but living conditions in the city did not improve. Food was in short supply and many citizens died.

Boston's prospects brightened in March 1776, when General Washington seized two hills in the town of Dorchester. The hills overlooked Boston Harbor. From their summits, Washington's cannons could easily target the fleet of British warships anchored in the harbor.

The British had two choices: They could either try to retake the hills or leave Boston without a fight. They decided to leave. The fleet sailed out of Boston Harbor on March 17, taking General Howe and many British loyalists with it. Before the British ships were out of sight, hundreds of refugees from Boston — including the Revere family — had already begun to move back.

Those returning found much of the city in shambles. Trees had been cut down for fuel and even the Old South Meeting House had been stripped of its pews and pulpit. Many rebel homes had been looted by the occupying army before the British left. Fortunately, Paul's house and shop were intact. His son Paul Jr. had done a good job of protecting them.

Dr. Joseph Warren's body had been missing ever since his death in the Battle of Bunker Hill. Now that the British were gone, Warren's two brothers and Paul sailed across the harbor to Charlestown in search of the doctor's remains. Once they'd found and identified them, they planned to rebury their brother and friend in a proper grave.

Luckily it didn't take them long to locate where Warren was buried, but his body was badly decomposed. They weren't even sure it was Warren's until Paul made a positive identification. He recognized the two false teeth he had made for his friend a few years before.

Dr. Joseph Warren in the uniform of a major general that he wore during the fighting at Breed's Hill.

An overflow crowd, including Paul, filled King's Chapel for Dr. Warren's funeral on April 8, 1776. A year later, Rachel Revere gave birth to a baby boy. His parents named him Joseph Warren Revere, in memory of his father's dear friend.

Paul Revere, who was now forty-one, made no more rides for the Revolution. The new Continental army had express riders of its own that it could send in his place. But Paul continued to show his support in different ways. His first assignment came a few days after Joseph Warren's funeral.

9

$\mathcal{D}$EFEAT

$\mathcal{T}$HE BRITISH HAD LEFT BOSTON, BUT GENERAL WASHINGTON was convinced that they planned to come back. To prepare for their return, Paul was asked to assemble a team and sail out to Castle Island in Boston Harbor. The British had damaged the island's cannons before they sailed away, but Washington believed the weapons could be repaired. Paul not only restored the cannons, but he invented better gun carriages for them to rest upon.

Soon Washington and most of his army left Boston for New York City, where they hoped to dislodge the British occupiers. In the future, Boston would have to organize its own defense. Paul joined the city's militia with the rank of major and was assigned to "maintain and take command of Castle Island." He didn't see any fighting there, however, since the British fleet never returned.

Along with his military duties, Paul again took charge of his shop. He was glad to be back making silver plates and pitchers — objects that had earned him the reputation of being the finest master craftsman in America. But sadness also touched him and his family. In May 1777, after a long illness, Paul's mother, Deborah, died at the age of seventy-three. She left a gaping hole in the household where she had lived ever since her husband's death twenty-three years earlier.

As the Revolutionary War continued, the bulk of the fighting occurred in the Middle Atlantic colonies — New Jersey, Pennsylvania, Maryland, and Virginia. But

A sharp-eyed Paul is shown in his workshop in this well-known portrait from life by John Singleton Copley.

there were also some clashes in New England, and Paul took part in several of them. In August 1778, he commanded the Boston artillery in an expedition to free Newport, Rhode Island, from British occupation.

Everyone in the expedition hoped for success since France, which had joined forces with the colonies, had sent a fleet to support the American attack from the sea. But a great storm severely damaged the French ships, putting them out of action. As a result, General John Hancock decided his American troops stood no chance against the superior British force defending Newport. The Americans, including Paul Revere, returned home in defeat.

A year later, in August 1779, Paul took part in another ill-fated expedition. This one was intended to capture a naval base the British had established on Penobscot Bay in Castine, Maine. Again, Paul commanded the Boston artillery on one of the American ships that sailed up along the Atlantic coast to Castine.

The American force reached Castine, bravely stormed a height opposite the base, and got their artillery in place. They were deciding what to do next when four British ships arrived unexpectedly on the scene. Caught by surprise, the Americans wilted as the British attacked from the rear. Some of the American ships were blown up by their own crews to prevent them from falling into the hands of the British. Others ran aground, and a few fled up the Penobscot River.

In the confusion, Paul lost his ship and became separated from most of the men under his command. Only later did he locate them, and together they started walking back to Boston under a hot August sun. Never had Paul experienced such a humiliating defeat.

Worse was yet to come. When Paul finally reached Boston, he was accused of unsoldier-like behavior and cowardice during the expedition. He was discharged from his command at Castle Island and told to remain at home while the authorities launched an investigation into his case. Paul was determined to clear his name. He wrote to the investigators, asking to meet his accusers face-to-face in a court-martial. While awaiting a reply, he and his son Paul Jr. went back to work in the Revere shop.

The Revolutionary War dragged on for two more years, and so did Paul Revere's search for justice. At last, on October 19, 1781, the British Lord Cornwallis surrendered to General George Washington in Yorktown, Virginia. And in February 1782, Paul was given the trial he had been seeking for so long.

Twelve naval captains considered the two charges against him. After several days of deliberation, they announced their verdict.

The British surrendering their Arms to Gen. Washington after their defeat at York Town in Virginia October 1781.

General George Washington, center left, accepts the surrender of the British commander Lord Cornwallis, center right, in this painting by an artist of the time.

Paul was acquitted of both charges. He had persevered, and his reputation had been restored.

When the final peace treaty with Great Britain was signed in 1783, and the colonies officially won their independence, Paul Revere was forty-eight years old. Another man that age might have been content to bask in what he had already achieved. After all, he had played a major role in helping his country win its independence. And he had built a successful business as a silversmith.

Paul Revere wasn't just any man, though. Nor were all his important accomplishments behind him. In fact, some of the most important lay ahead.

Before the Revolution, the colonies had to import most of their manufactured goods — everything from plows to church bells — from Great Britain. Now that America had won its independence, American craftsmen were free to make whatever they wanted.

Paul Revere was one of the first people to take advantage of this new freedom.

While continuing to run his silversmith shop, he set up a foundry amid Boston's shipyards in 1788. "We have got our furnass agoing," he wrote excitedly to a friend. And soon the foundry was turning out a steady supply of iron hammers, anvils, and stoves.

Business was good, but Paul had even more ambitious plans for his foundry. The bells in Boston's many churches often needed to be repaired or replaced. Before, this work had always been done in faroff Eng-

land. But when a bell in Revere's own church cracked in 1792, Paul convinced the church leaders that he could repair it right there in Boston.

In fact, Paul knew nothing about bell-casting. However, he had heard of a man in the Boston area who had cast bells in England. With the man's help, and 912 pounds of molten copper, tin, zinc, and lead, Paul made a mold for the huge bell and cast it successfully. Before the bell cooled, he put

This 900-pound bell, dated 1804, is one of twenty-three bells known to exist that were cast during the time Paul Revere was personally involved with his foundry. It can be seen today in the courtyard of the Revere House in Boston.

a simple inscription on it: "The first bell cast in Boston 1792 P. Revere."

In the years that followed, Paul and his son Joseph Warren cast more than a hundred bells for churches all over New England. They made other bells for churches as far away as Savannah, Georgia, and Havana, Cuba. Paul wrote proudly, "We have never heard that any one has been broken or received any complaint of the sound." But he already had his eye on new business opportunities.

America had started to assemble a navy, and one of its new ships, the *Constitution*, was to be built in Boston's shipyard. Paul wrote to the officials in charge saying he could make its metal fittings — "composition bolts, rudder braces, etc." — in his foundry. "I will do them as cheap as anyone and as well."

The U.S.S. Constitution, *for which Paul made a copper bottom.*

Paul got the commission, but there was one thing he could not make for the *Constitution* — its copper bottom. Every large ship needed one to protect it from the barnacles that attached themselves to a wooden bottom and reduced the ship's speed. But the sheet copper required for the bottoms still had to be imported from England. No one in America had the equipment to make it.

Paul was determined to change that. He had always gotten his greatest satisfaction from making fine and useful things, whether they be handsome silver plates or perfectly tuned church bells. Now, at age sixty-five, he decided to build a rolling mill that could produce sheet copper. It would be the first such mill in America — and very expensive. "It will require every farthing I can rake and scrape," he confessed to a friend.

First, he obtained a U.S. government bank loan of $10,000. With that in hand, he purchased a site for the mill in Canton, Massachusetts, near the powder factory he had built earlier. The site was on a branch of the Neponset River, which would provide the necessary water power for the mill.

Next, he risked $25,000 of his own money — almost everything he had — to construct the mill and equip it with top-quality rollers imported from England. It was a daring gamble. What if the mill, on completion, produced inferior sheet copper? He would be ruined.

A chalk drawing of Paul in profile at age sixty-five, made by the French artist Balthazar Julien Fevret de Saint-memin. Saint-memin used a device known as a physiognotrace, a sort of stylus, to trace the outline of Paul's head, and transfer the outline to paper.

Paul had never shied away from a challenge, though. Nor had he ever been afraid of trying new things. He had mastered every skill he set out to learn, from making false teeth to engraving copper plates to casting church bells. But before he could add another accomplishment to the list, word came that George Washington had died on December 14, 1799.

10

SADNESS AND SUCCESS

Gold urn made by Paul Revere to hold a lock of the late George Washington's hair.

PAUL — AND THE NATION — WERE PLUNGED INTO GRIEF BY the loss of the great leader and former president. In Boston, the St. Andrew's Masonic Lodge made plans to honor Washington, their fellow Mason.

Three former Grand Masters of the Lodge, including Paul Revere, wrote a note of condolence to Martha Washington. In it, they requested a lock of Washington's hair to keep as an "invaluable relic of the Hero and Patriot."

Mrs. Washington was happy to oblige. She knew the part her husband had played in freeing Boston from British occupation and his devotion to Masonic ideals. To house the lock, Paul Revere made one of his most beautiful objects. It was a small golden urn, three and seven-eighths inches tall, mounted upon a mahogany base. The top of the urn could be opened, and inside, under a protective sheet of glass, rested the lock of Washington's hair.

Paul's urn was just one of the ways Boston Masons paid tribute to George Washington's memory. On February 11, 1800, they staged a grand procession through the streets of the city. It started from the Old State House at ten in the morning, and ended back there at five in the afternoon. Hundreds of Bostonians, from babes in arms to elderly people on canes, watched from the sidelines as the paraders marched past.

The climax came when a replica of Paul's golden urn, three feet high and made of "artificial marble," appeared on a wagon draped in black crepe. Six pallbearers accompanied the wagon, three on each side. One of them was Paul Revere.

Later in 1800, Paul sold his house on North Square — the Revere House that school groups and tourists visit today. He bought a new and bigger house on Charter Street, and moved into it with his wife, Rachel, and their five living children.

The Reveres did not spend all their time in the new house. During the summer, they moved to a small house in Canton that Paul had acquired along with land for his rolling mill. Paul still kept a horse, and in good weather he liked to ride it for exercise.

A drawing, possibly sketched by Paul, showing his copper mill (buildings left and right) and home (center) in Canton, Massachusetts.

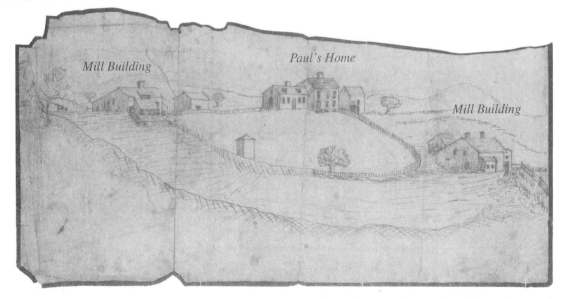

Mill Building

Paul's Home

Mill Building

The Massachusetts State House in Boston as it looks today. Its dome was covered with sheet copper made by Paul, and later gilded.

In 1801, the mill was ready to open at last. Once again Paul was concerned about its prospects. Would the copper the mill produced be up to world standards? He needn't have worried. A short time after the mill started production, he wrote proudly to a friend, "I have erected my Works & have Rolled Sheet Copper which is approved of by the best judges. . . ."

Orders quickly followed. The first big one was for 6,000 feet of sheet copper to cover the dome of the New State House in Boston. Sixty years later the dome was gild-ed with gold leaf, and it still glitters on the Boston skyline today. But Paul's steadiest orders came from shipbuilders. When the original copper bottom of the *Constitution* was replaced in 1803, the Revere rolling mill got the job.

By now the mill was employing fifty or so full-time workers. Paul paid the men more than the going rate — about two dollars a day. But he wanted his employees to be con-tent, he wrote in a letter, and believed that better pay would result in better work.

A bad storm in the fall of 1804 blew the

roof off the foundry in Boston where Paul and his son cast bells. Rather than rebuild it, Paul decided to move the foundry to Canton near the rolling mill. At about the same time, he stopped working as a silversmith. He was seventy now and had his hands full managing both the foundry and the rolling mill.

By 1805, most American men were wearing trousers and hats with brims. But Paul still favored the knee britches and three-cornered hats that were customary during the Revolution. Small boys sometimes snickered when they saw him walk by in his old-fashioned clothes.

Paul's clothes may have been behind the times, but his thinking was not. In 1809, he joined forces with Robert Fulton, inventor of some of the first steamboats. Fulton's boats and others like them promised to revolutionize river and ocean transportation. No longer would people be dependent on oars or an uncertain wind to propel their boats forward.

But steamboats were only as good as the boilers that generated their power. The boilers presently in use often failed to function, and sometimes they exploded. To guard against this, Paul manufactured thick copper sheets for use in the boilers on Robert Fulton's ships. Once installed, they racked up an impressive safety record.

In 1811, Paul Revere retired from day-to-day management of his copper mill. His son

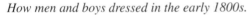

How men and boys dressed in the early 1800s.

Joseph Warren assumed most of his father's duties. Now that he had more time to rest and relax, Paul wrote a poem about life in his country home, Canton Dale. Here is how he described his morning routine:

> *At early morn I take my round,*
> *Invited first by hammer's sound;*
> *The Furnace next; then Rolling-Mill;*
> *'Till Breakfast's call'd, my time doth fill;*
> *Then round my Acres (few) I trot,*
> *To see what's done and what is not. . . .*

Paul's pleasant life in Canton Dale was interrupted on June 18, 1812, when the United States once again declared war on Great Britain. This time the fight was triggered by British attacks on United States ships and the seizure of American seamen.

Everyone in Massachusetts expected that Boston would eventually be attacked from the sea. Even though he was seventy-nine, Paul was among the first to volunteer to help build more forts in Boston Harbor in 1814.

Fortunately, the forts were never needed. During the war, the British occupied Washington briefly and burned the White House and other government buildings. British naval vessels also raided shore towns up and down the Atlantic coast, from Maryland to Maine. But Boston, for some reason, was spared. When the war finally ended with a peace treaty in 1815, the citizens of Boston rejoiced at their good fortune.

Paul rejoiced with them, but probably in a quiet way. He was still mourning the loss of his beloved wife, Rachel, who had died on June 26, 1813, at the age of sixty-seven. Rachel Revere was interred in the Granary Burying Ground in the heart of Boston. Her grave was not far from those of Paul's first wife, Sara, and his father, Apollos Rivoire.

Meanwhile, Paul himself lived on, as mentally alert and physically sturdy as ever. But the years were passing, and in 1816, when he was eighty-one, he made his will. He had fathered sixteen children, eight with Sara and eight more with Rachel, but only five were still living. Paul provided generously for each of them and left the copper mill to his son Joseph Warren, who had been his father's chief assistant for many years.

Earlier in 1816, the largest bell the Revere foundry had ever cast was hung in the tower of King's Chapel in Boston. It was known as "the passing bell" because it was rung whenever someone in the city died. Before long it would toll for the man who had made it.

Paul Revere at age seventy-eight in early June 1813. His son Joseph Warren Revere paid the American artist Gilbert Stuart $200 for this painting and the accompanying portrait of Joseph's mother, Rachel.

Rachel Revere was sixty-seven years old when she sat for her portrait. She died on June 26, 1813, several weeks after the painting was finished.

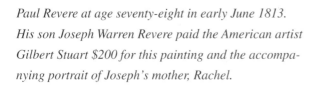

11

Cool
IN THOUGHT,
ARDENT
IN ACTION

Paul Revere passed away on May 10, 1818, at the age of eighty-three. In a time when most men died in their forties and fifties, this was the equivalent of someone today living to be a hundred and ten or more.

Boston's newspapers paid tribute to Paul with lengthy obituaries. The *Boston Intelligencer* summed up his life in these words: "Cool in thought, ardent in action, he was well adapted to form plans, and to carry them into execution — both for the benefit of himself & the service of others. . . ."

Another newspaper called him "one of the earliest and most indefatigable Patriots and Soldiers of the Revolution."

A third commented: "Seldom has the tomb closed upon a life so honourable and useful."

Today most people know of Paul Revere mainly through the poem "Paul Revere's Ride" by Henry Wadsworth Longfellow. Published in January 1861, a few months before the start of the Civil War, it was

Paul Revere's grave marker in Boston's Granary Burying Ground.

meant to inspire readers by reminding them of Paul's heroic deed.

But his midnight ride was only one of Paul Revere's achievements, and not necessarily the most important. His skills as a silversmith set the standard for every American craftsman who followed him. The many other rides he made on behalf of the Revolution played a key role in America's eventually winning its independence. After the war, his manufacture of church bells and sheet copper were prime examples of early American industrialization.

Finally, like millions of other Americans, Paul Revere showed in his life and work just how far the child of an immigrant could go.

Photograph of Henry Wadsworth Longfellow in old age.

"Paul Revere's Ride"
The Poem and Its Author

Henry Wadsworth Longfellow (1807–1882) was one of the most popular American poets in the middle years of the nineteenth century. He was best known for poems like "Evangeline," "The Song of Hiawatha," and "The Courtship of Miles Standish" that told dramatic stories in clear, vivid language. Then, in 1860, he wrote what would become one of his most famous works, "Paul Revere's Ride."

Most Americans had not heard of Paul Revere when Longfellow sat down to write his poem. But Longfellow lived in Cambridge, Massachusetts, where old-timers still told tales of Revere's ride on that April night in 1775. The poet was deeply troubled in 1860 by all the talk of Civil War that swirled around him. He wanted to write something that would remind his countrymen of their heroic Revolutionary past, when Americans from North and South had joined forces to declare their independence from Great Britain and build a new country. A poetic account of Paul Revere's ride seemed the perfect way to transmit his message.

Longfellow's poem was published in a Boston literary magazine, *The Atlantic Monthly*, in January 1861. A few months later, Southern forces fired on Fort Sumter and the Civil War began. There's no way to prove whether the poem inspired Northern readers to be more patriotic in the bloody years that followed. But one thing is certain: "Paul Revere's Ride" brought lasting fame and renown to its main character.

Paul Revere's Ride

By Henry Wadsworth Longfellow

[1860, first published 1861]

Listen, my children, and you shall hear
Of the midnight ride of Paul Revere,
On the eighteenth of April, in Seventy-Five;
Hardly a man is now alive
Who remembers that famous day and year.

He said to his friend, "If the British march
By land or sea from the town to-night,
Hang a lantern aloft in the belfry arch
Of the North Church tower, as a signal light,—
One, if by land, and two, if by sea;
And I on the opposite shore will be,
Ready to ride and spread the alarm
Through every Middlesex village and farm,
For the country folk to be up and to arm."

Then he said "Good-night!" and with muffled oar
Silently rowed to the Charlestown shore,
Just as the moon rose over the bay,
Where swinging wide at her moorings lay
The *Somerset*, British man-of-war;
A phantom ship, with each mast and spar
Across the moon like a prison-bar,
And a huge black hulk, that was magnified
By its own reflection in the tide.

Meanwhile, his friend, through alley and street
Wanders and watches with eager ears,
Till in the silence around him he hears
The muster of men at the barrack door,
The sound of arms, and the tramp of feet,

And the measured tread of the grenadiers,
Marching down to their boats on the shore.
Then he climbed the tower of the Old North Church,
By the wooden stairs, with stealthy tread,
To the belfry-chamber overhead,
And startled the pigeons from their perch
On the somber rafters, that round him made
Masses and moving shapes of shade,—
By the trembling ladder, steep and tall,
To the highest window in the wall,
Where he paused to listen and look down
A moment on the roofs of the town,
And the moonlight flowing over all.

Beneath, in the churchyard, lay the dead,
In their night-encampment on the hill,
Wrapped in silence so deep and still
That he could hear, like a sentinel's tread,
The watchful night-wind, as it went

Creeping along from tent to tent,
And seeming to whisper, "All is well!"
A moment only he feels the spell
Of the place and the hour, and the secret dread
Of the lonely belfry and the dead;
For suddenly all his thoughts are bent
On a shadowy something far away,
Where the river widens to meet the bay,—
A line of black, that bends and floats
On the rising tide, like a bridge of boats.

Meanwhile, impatient to mount and ride,
Booted and spurred, with a heavy stride
On the opposite shore walked Paul Revere.
Now he patted his horse's side,
Now gazed on the landscape far and near,
Then, impetuous, stamped the earth,
And turned and tightened his saddle-girth;
But mostly he watched with eager search
The belfry-tower of the Old North Church,
As it rose above the graves on the hill,
Lonely and spectral and somber and still.
And lo! as he looks, on the belfry's height
A glimmer, and then a gleam of light!
He springs to the saddle, the bridle he turns,
But lingers and gazes, till full on his sight
A second lamp in the belfry burns!

A hurry of hoofs in a village street,
A shape in the moonlight, a bulk in the dark,
And beneath, from the pebbles, in passing, a spark
Struck out by a steed flying fearless and fleet:
That was all! And yet, through the gloom and the light,
The fate of a nation was riding that night;
And the spark struck out by that steed, in his flight,
Kindled the land into flame with its heat.

He has left the village and mounted the steep,
And beneath him, tranquil and broad and deep,
Is the Mystic, meeting the ocean tides;
And under the alders that skirt its edge,
Now soft on the sand, now loud on the ledge,
Is heard the tramp of his steed as he rides.

It was twelve by the village clock,
When he crossed the bridge into Medford town.
He heard the crowing of the cock,
And the barking of the farmer's dog,
And felt the damp of the river fog,
That rises after the sun goes down.

It was one by the village clock,
When he galloped into Lexington.
He saw the gilded weathercock
Swim in the moonlight as he passed,
And the meeting-house windows, blank and bare,
Gaze at him with a spectral glare,
As if they already stood aghast
At the bloody work they would look upon.

It was two by the village clock,

When he came to the bridge in Concord town.

He heard the bleating of the flock,

And the twitter of birds among the trees,

And felt the breath of the morning breeze

Blowing over the meadow brown.

And one was safe and asleep in his bed

Who at the bridge would be first to fall,

Who that day would be lying dead,

Pierced by a British musket-ball.

You know the rest. In the books you have read,

How the British regulars fired and fled,—

How the farmers gave them ball for ball,

From behind each fence and farm-yard wall,

Chasing the red-coats down the lane,

Then crossing the fields to emerge again

Under the trees at the turn of the road,

And only pausing to fire and load.

So through the night rode Paul Revere;

And so through the night went his cry of alarm

To every Middlesex village and farm,—

A cry of defiance, and not of fear,

A voice in the darkness, a knock at the door,

And a word that shall echo for evermore!

For, borne on the night-wind of the Past,

Through all our history, to the last,

In the hour of darkness and peril and need,

The people will waken and listen to hear

The hurrying hoof-beat of that steed,

And the midnight message of Paul Revere.

A Comparison

*I*f you compare the events in the poem with the account of Revere's ride in Chapter 6, you'll spot a number of striking differences. For example, Longfellow omits any mention of the other rider, William Dawes. He obviously wants the focus to remain solely on Paul and his brave actions that night.

Once he is on the road to Lexington, Paul doesn't have to detour around British guards. And when he finally gets to Lexington, he doesn't stop to warn Samuel Adams and John Hancock that the British are on the way. Instead, he rides straight on toward Concord.

In the poem, Paul reaches Concord without any trouble. But in reality, as we've seen, he and William Dawes and a young doctor riding with them were halted on the road to Concord by a band of British guards.

Revere, Dawes, and the doctor all tried to make a break for it. In the ensuing struggle, Dawes lost his horse and Paul was recaptured after six more guards suddenly appeared in front of him. Only Dr. Prescott managed to elude the British and make his way to Concord.

You can find a number of other places where the poet deviates from the facts of Paul's ride. But if challenged, Longfellow would probably say that he did it deliberately. His aim wasn't to write an accurate historical account of the night's events but to transform the real Paul Revere into a valiant hero and his midnight ride into an American legend. Judging by the enduring impact his poem has had over the past century and a half, Longfellow more than achieved his goal.

Paul Revere
Time Line

Apollos Rivoire arrives in Boston at age thirteen and is apprenticed to goldsmith John Coney.

Apollos Rivoire changes his name to Paul Revere, marries Deborah Hitchbourn, and opens his own firm, "Paul Revere, Goldsmith & Silversmith."

1716 **1730**

On returning to Boston, Paul, now twenty-two, marries Sara Orne. They live with Paul's mother in the Revere house near Clark's Wharf.

Paul is recognized as a master goldsmith and makes fine silverware for wealthy merchants. In April, his first child, Deborah, is born.

Paul joins St. Andrew's Masonic Lodge, where he begins a lifelong friendship with Dr. Joseph Warren. He also becomes a member of the Long Room Club, a discussion group that includes the city's leading thinkers, including Samuel Adams and John Hancock. In January, his first son, Paul, is born.

The British Parliament passes the Stamp Act. Paul uses his engraving skills to produce cartoons opposing the Act.

Paul studies dentistry and becomes a dentist as well as a silversmith. He makes the famous Liberty Bowl, and continues to engrave political cartoons.

1757 **1758** **1760** **1765** **1768**

At the rebel leaders' request, Paul builds a gunpowder mill in Canton, Massachusetts, near Boston, to supply the troops of the new American army.

After seven attempts, Paul finally obtains a court-martial so that he can answer charges made against him following the Penobscot expedition. He is honorably acquitted. The peace treaty with Great Britain is signed, in 1783, and America formally wins its independence.

On April 18, at age forty, Paul makes his famous midnight ride to alert the country-side of a planned British march to Lexington and Concord. Later in 1775, Paul engraves and prints desperately needed paper money for the colonies.

Paul assumes command of the fortress on Castle Island in Boston Harbor. His son Joseph Warren Revere is born; his mother, Deborah, dies.

Paul commands the ship carrying the artillery in a failed American expedition against the British in Penobscot Bay, Maine.

1775 **1776** **1777** **1779** **1782**

To protect it against damage from barnacles and shipworms, the hull of the *Constitution* is plated with Revere copper.

At age seventy-five, Paul makes copper for the boilers of steamboats designed by inventor Robert Fulton.

Paul's mill manufactures copper sheeting for the dome of the new State House in Boston.

In their old age, Paul and Rachel Revere have their portraits painted by the artist Gilbert Stuart. Rachel dies several weeks later on June 26.

1802 **1803** **1809** **1813**

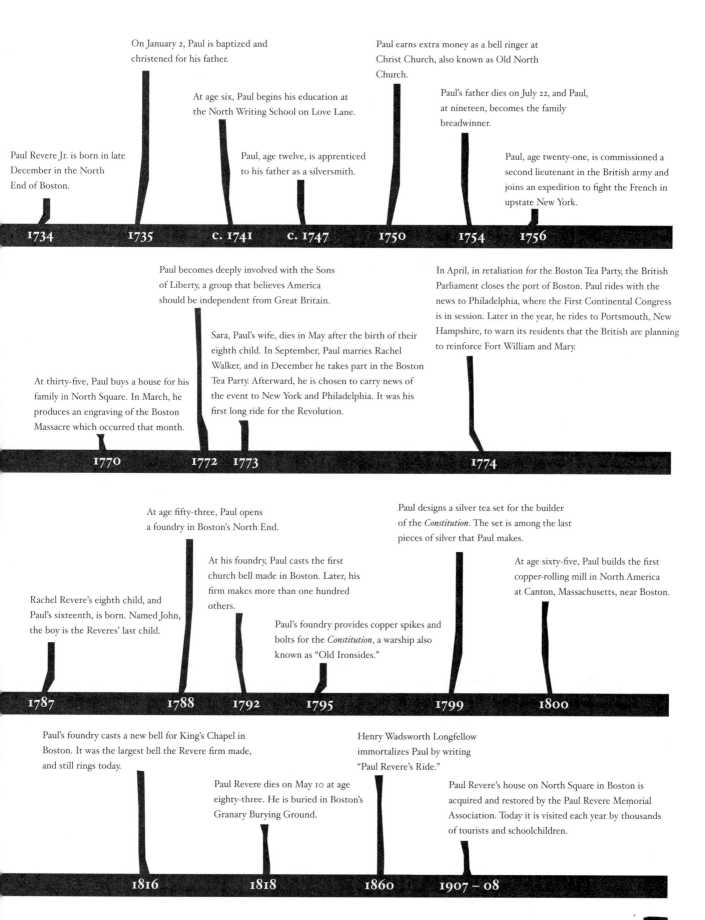

On January 2, Paul is baptized and christened for his father.

At age six, Paul begins his education at the North Writing School on Love Lane.

Paul earns extra money as a bell ringer at Christ Church, also known as Old North Church.

Paul's father dies on July 22, and Paul, at nineteen, becomes the family breadwinner.

Paul Revere Jr. is born in late December in the North End of Boston.

Paul, age twelve, is apprenticed to his father as a silversmith.

Paul, age twenty-one, is commissioned a second lieutenant in the British army and joins an expedition to fight the French in upstate New York.

1734   1735   c. 1741   c. 1747   1750   1754   1756

Paul becomes deeply involved with the Sons of Liberty, a group that believes America should be independent from Great Britain.

In April, in retaliation for the Boston Tea Party, the British Parliament closes the port of Boston. Paul rides with the news to Philadelphia, where the First Continental Congress is in session. Later in the year, he rides to Portsmouth, New Hampshire, to warn its residents that the British are planning to reinforce Fort William and Mary.

Sara, Paul's wife, dies in May after the birth of their eighth child. In September, Paul marries Rachel Walker, and in December he takes part in the Boston Tea Party. Afterward, he is chosen to carry news of the event to New York and Philadelphia. It was his first long ride for the Revolution.

At thirty-five, Paul buys a house for his family in North Square. In March, he produces an engraving of the Boston Massacre which occurred that month.

1770   1772   1773   1774

At age fifty-three, Paul opens a foundry in Boston's North End.

Paul designs a silver tea set for the builder of the *Constitution*. The set is among the last pieces of silver that Paul makes.

At his foundry, Paul casts the first church bell made in Boston. Later, his firm makes more than one hundred others.

At age sixty-five, Paul builds the first copper-rolling mill in North America at Canton, Massachusetts, near Boston.

Rachel Revere's eighth child, and Paul's sixteenth, is born. Named John, the boy is the Reveres' last child.

Paul's foundry provides copper spikes and bolts for the *Constitution*, a warship also known as "Old Ironsides."

1787   1788   1792   1795   1799   1800

Paul's foundry casts a new bell for King's Chapel in Boston. It was the largest bell the Revere firm made, and still rings today.

Henry Wadsworth Longfellow immortalizes Paul by writing "Paul Revere's Ride."

Paul Revere dies on May 10 at age eighty-three. He is buried in Boston's Granary Burying Ground.

Paul Revere's house on North Square in Boston is acquired and restored by the Paul Revere Memorial Association. Today it is visited each year by thousands of tourists and schoolchildren.

1816   1818   1860   1907 – 08

Historic Sites to Visit

Would you like to visit the house where Paul Revere lived and follow the route of his midnight ride? If you're ever in the vicinity of Boston, Massachusetts, you can, for almost all of the sites associated with Paul have been preserved and are open to visitors.

BOSTON

In Boston, you can follow the three-mile-long **Freedom Trail**, which winds through the center of the city. It begins at an information center on Boston Common near the intersection of Tremont Street and Temple Place. A red line, sometimes painted on the sidewalk and sometimes formed of red bricks, leads from one place to another along the Trail. The line helps make sure you won't get lost.

Boston Common was the park where British soldiers camped when they were sent to occupy the city after the Boston Tea Party. It was also the place where British troops mustered before rowing across the Charles River to Cambridge on the night of April 18, 1775.

Across the Common, at the top of Beacon Hill, is the **Massachusetts State House** (Beacon Street, Boston, MA 02133). If it's a nice day, the dome that

Paul Revere covered with copper, and that was later gilded, will be glittering in the sun.

From the State House, the Trail leads down Park Street and turns left on Tremont Street to the **Granary Burying Ground** (83-115 Tremont Street, Boston, MA 02108). Many prominent Bostonians are buried here. As you stroll along the paths, you'll come to the graves of John Hancock, Samuel Adams, and Paul Revere among others. The Burying Ground is also the final resting place of the victims of the Boston Massacre.

The Trail continues on past the Old City Hall to the **Old South Meeting House** (310 Washington Street, Boston, MA 02108). A meeting of revolutionaries took place here shortly before the Boston Tea Party.

The next stop on the Trail is the **Old State House** (206 Washington Street, Boston, MA 02109). A circle of cobblestones in the street outside the building marks the spot where the Boston Massacre occurred.

Beyond the Old State House, the Trail circles around **Faneuil** (pronounced Fannel) **Hall**, which came to be known as the "Cradle of Liberty" because of the many protests against British policy that were voiced in its meeting rooms.

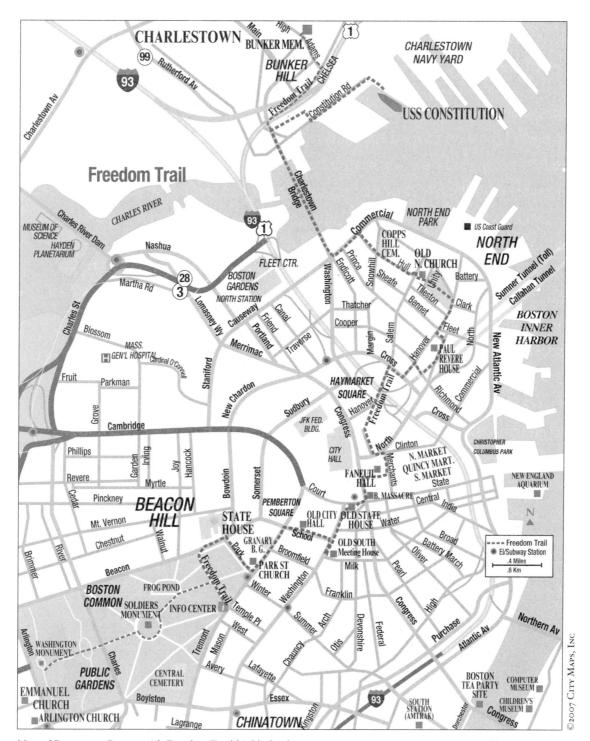

Map of Downtown Boston with Freedom Trail highlighted.

The Trail continues into Boston's North End, the oldest part of the city. After you walk a few blocks farther, you'll come to one of the most popular sites on the Trail, **Paul Revere's House** (19 North Square, Boston, MA 02113). Built about 1680, it is the oldest surviving house in Boston. It was Paul's home from 1770 until 1800. One room in the house is furnished with artifacts from the time of the first owner, Robert Howard, a wealthy Puritan merchant. The three other historic rooms contain furnishings from Paul's day, including Revere family furniture and silver made in Paul's shop.

It's just a short walk to the next stop on the Trail, the **Old North Church** (193 Salem Street, Boston MA 02113). Old North, built in 1723 and also known as Christ Church, Episcopal, is the oldest church building in Boston. It's the church whose bells Paul rang as a boy. From its steeple, still one of the tallest in the city, two lanterns were hung on the night of April 18-19, 1775, to warn the people of Charlestown that British troops would be crossing the harbor.

From the Old North Church, the Trail continues past historic Copps Hill Cemetery, and then descends the hill to the Charlestown Bridge across Boston Harbor. You can follow the Trail on foot across the bridge, but it's a long hike. You may prefer to travel to the sites in Charlestown by car instead. Public transportation is also available.

CHARLESTOWN

The last two sites on the Freedom Trail are both located in Charlestown. The first is the **U.S.S. Constitution**, for which Paul made the copper sheeting that protected its bottom, or hull. (The warship is berthed in the Boston Naval Shipyard, Charlestown, MA 02129.) Launched in 1797, the *Constitution* got the nickname "Old Ironsides" because cannonballs shot at it in battle reputedly bounced off its thick wooden sides. Free tours of the ship are conducted regularly by young Navy enlistees.

The final stop on the Trail is the **Bunker Hill Monument** (Monument Square, Charlestown, MA 02129). It is actually located atop Breed's Hill, where the fighting known as the Battle of Bunker Hill took place. Construction of the monument, built in the form of an obelisk, was begun in 1827 but wasn't completed until 1843.

After you've seen all the sites on the Freedom Trail, you'll want to go on — if you have the time — to explore the sites outside Boston that played a role in Paul's famed midnight ride. You can reach some of them by bus or train, but to see them all, you'll need to go by car.

LEXINGTON AND CONCORD

(For map showing Lexington and Concord, and their relationship to Boston, see page 39.)

Located eleven miles northwest of Boston, the town of **Lexington** contains many sites closely associated with the midnight ride. Most of them are within easy walking distance of one another.

Any visit should start at the **Lexington Visitor's Center** (1875 Massachusetts Avenue) which offers information and hospitality to tourists. The center is directly across from the **Battle Green** where the first fighting in the Revolutionary War took place.

As you walk across the green, you'll see the **Minuteman Statue**. Erected in 1900, the statue memorializes the brave militiamen who assembled on the green to confront the approaching British troops. Also situated on the green is the **Revolutionary Monument**. It was unveiled on July 4, 1799, and is the oldest war memorial in the United States. Close by it are buried the remains of the eight minutemen who were slain in the Battle of Lexington on April 19, 1775.

Across from the Battle Green, you can visit the **Buckman Tavern** (1 Bedford Street). The tavern, built between 1704 and 1710, is the oldest one in Lexington. It's the tavern from which Paul Revere rescued John Han-

cock's trunk just before fighting broke out on the green. The building has been carefully preserved and looks much as it did in Paul's time.

A short distance from the Buckman Tavern is the **Hancock-Clarke House**. Paul Revere rode to this house on the night of April 18-19, 1775, to warn Samuel Adams and John Hancock, who were staying there, that the British were on their way to Lexington. Today the house, built about 1738, is administered by the Lexington Historical Society and contains furnishings from the Revolutionary era.

Your last stop in Lexington will probably be the visitor center of the **Minute Man National Historical Park**, located just outside town on Route 2A. Organized and maintained by the National Park Service, the park's goal is to preserve and protect the significant historic sites, buildings, and landscapes associated with the opening battles of the American Revolution. It consists of more than 900 acres of land within the towns of Lexington, Lincoln, and Concord, Massachusetts.

The park's acres include many segments of the **Battle Road** that was the scene of hand-to-hand fighting during the British retreat from Concord and Lexington on April 19, 1775. Today, a five-mile-long hiking trail incorporates the surviving parts of the road along which the British retreated. Other sections of the trail explore the parallel route the Americans took through fields and woods as they pursued the British.

If you've decided to hike the trail from Lexington toward Concord, you'll soon come to the **Paul Revere Capture Site**—the place where British guards intercepted Paul in the early morning hours of April 19, 1775. If you're traveling the eleven-mile distance between the two towns by car, you can still see the Capture Site; it's not far off Route 2A and is clearly marked.

In **Concord**, the most important Revolutionary War site is the **North Bridge**. This is the bridge where determined American militiamen confronted the oncoming British redcoats, and forced them to retreat. The poet Ralph Waldo Emerson, who lived in Concord, immortalized their encounter — the first major battle in the American Revolution — with these words:

> *By the rude bridge that arched the flood,*
> *Their flag to April's breeze unfurled,*
> *Here once the embattled farmers stood,*
> *And fired the shot heard round the world.*

If you're lucky enough to be in Massachusetts in mid-April, you may be able to take part in the **Patriot's Day reenactments** at Lexington and Concord. Patriot's Day celebrates the fighting that took place in and around the two historic towns on April 19, 1775. It is observed annually throughout Massachusetts on the third Monday in April.

The major events in the Patriot's Day celebrations include a reenactment of the skirmish between the Lexington militia and British troops on Lexington Green; another reenactment of the capture of Paul Revere by British guards near the town of Lincoln; and a third reenactment of the historic clash of American and British forces at the North Bridge in Concord.

Watching these reenactments — and walking the Freedom Trail — will help to transport you back to Paul Revere's time. You'll walk the same narrow Boston streets that he walked, and travel the route he traveled to help the rebels of Lexington and Concord prepare themselves for the fighting to come.

Source Notes and Bibliography

Two books were especially helpful as I delved into Paul Revere's life and what really happened on his midnight ride. Both of them draw heavily on Paul Revere's own accounts of the ride, which are among the Revere Family Papers held by the Massachusetts Historical Society in Boston.

The two books are: *Paul Revere and the World He Lived In* by Esther Forbes. Boston and New York: Houghton Mifflin Company, 1942; Mariner Books (an imprint of Houghton Mifflin) paperback edition, 1999.

Paul Revere's Ride by David Hackett Fischer. New York: Oxford University Press, 1994; first Oxford paperback edition, 1995.

Other publications that provided useful information include an overall view of the American Revolution; two guidebooks to historic sites in Boston and vicinity; a book about Freemasonry (Paul Revere was a member of the Masonic Order); and a government pamphlet about early American money. Their titles are:

The American Revolution by Bruce Lancaster. New York: American Heritage, Inc., 1971; Boston, Mariner Books (an imprint of Houghton Mifflin Company) paperback edition, 2001.

Boston Sites and Insights by Susan Wilson. Boston: Beacon Press, 2004.

Uncommon Boston by Susan Berk with Jill Bloom. Reading, MA: Addison-Wesley Publishing Company, Inc., 1990.

Paul Revere and Freemasonry by Edith J. Steblecki. Boston: Paul Revere Memorial Association, 1985.

Money in Colonial Times. Booklet published by the Federal Reserve Bank of Philadelphia, 1989.

A number of Internet Web sites helped to fill in gaps in the research. The most useful were, in alphabetical order:

The City of Boston (www.cityofboston.gov). Visitor information on the "Freedom Trail" gives historical data on many of the sites mentioned, including the Massachusetts State House; the Granary Burying Ground, the Old South Meeting House, the Old North Church, the Old State House.

Colonial Williamsburg (www.history.org). Detailed information on a silversmith's craft can be found in the "Explore & Learn" section, under Experience the Life: Trades: Silversmith.

Copper Development Association (www.copper.org). The article "Old Ironsides Still Protected by Copper." can be found in Resources and Tools: Copper Topics: Fall 1977.

I Boston: Boston History and Architecture (www.iboston.org). This site provides detailed information on the sites, people, and events that played a key role in the Revolution.

The Masonic Service Association of North America (www.msana.com). Offers current and historical information in the "Learn About Freemasonry" link from the home page.

The Paul Revere House (www.paulreverehouse.org). This comprehensive site provides information on the house itself; a brief biography of Revere; details on "The Midnight Ride," including a copy of Longfellow's poem "Paul Revere's Ride"; the Revere Silver Shop, which includes examples of his work; and other topics relating to Paul Revere.

The United States Navy (www.ussconstitution.navy.mil). The official site for the U.S.S. *Constitution* ("Old Ironsides").

Illustration Credits

Cover, front: © 2007 Mark Summers

Cover, back, and page 86: Courtesy American Antiquarian Society, Worcester, MA

Page ii-iii: Courtesy of New York Public Library

Page vii: Courtesy of Paul Revere House

Frontispiece: Mary Evans Picture Library/The Image Works

Page 2: The Granger Collection, NY

Page 3: Bettmann/Corbis

Pages 4, 5: The Granger Collection, NY

Page 6, top left: Metropolitan Museum of Art; top right: Worcester Art Museum, Worcester, MA, Gift of the Paul Revere Insurance Co., a subsidiary of UnumProvident Co.; bottom: Collection, Paul Revere Memorial Association, Gift of Amory Goddard, in loving memory of his mother and father

Page 7: Bettmann/Corbis

Page 8: Massachusetts Historical Society

Page 10: Courtesy American Antiquarian Society

Page 11: Worcester Art Museum, Worcester, MA, Gift of William A. Savage

Page 12: Scholastic Photo Archive

Page 13: National Park Service, Archives, National Historical Parks

Page 14: The Granger Collection, NY

Page 15: Scholastic Photo Archive

Page 16: American Antiquarian Society, Worcester, MA/The Bridgeman Art Library

Page 17: Gift by Subscription and Francis Bartlett Fund, Museum of Fine Arts, Boston, MA/The Bridgeman Art Library

Pages 19, 21: Scholastic Photo Archive

Page 22: Paul Revere House

Page 23: Museum of Fine Arts, Boston

Pages 25, 26: Scholastic Photo Archive

Page 27: Metropolitan Museum of Art

Page 28: Collection, Paul Revere Memorial Association, Gift of M. W. Boyden

Page 29: Yale Center for British Art, Paul Mellon Collection, USA/The Bridgeman Art Library

Page 31: Bettmann/Corbis

Page 32: Courtesy Henry Cooke/Historical Costume Services

Page 34: The Granger Collection, NY

Page 36: Bettmann/Corbis

Page 37: Used with permission of the Paul Revere Life Insurance Company/Paul Revere House

Page 38: Scholastic Photo Archive

Page 39: Map by Richard Amari/Scholastic

Page 40: The Granger Collection, NY

Page 41: Courtesy Worcester Historical Museum, Worcester, MA

Page 43: Private Collection/The Bridgeman Art Library

Page 44: Superstock

Page 46: Scholastic Photo Archive

Page 47: Richard T. Nowitz/Corbis

Page 49: Painting by Don Troiani, www.historicalartprints.com

Page 50: Library of Congress (LC-USCZ4-4970)

Page 52: Library of Congress (LC-USZ62-27694)

Page 54: The Granger Collection, NY

Page 56: Library of Congress

Page 57: Paul Revere House

Page 58: The Granger Collection, NY

Page 59: Library of Congress (LC-USZ62-7407)

Page 60: Courtesy Grand Lodge of Massachusetts

Page 61: Massachusetts Historical Society

Page 62: David Sailors/Corbis

Page 63: The Granger Collection, NY

Page 65: Museum of Fine Arts, Boston

Page 67: Philippa Lewis; Edifice/Corbis

Page 68: The Museum of Modern Art/Licensed by SCALA/Art Resource

Page 77: Map of Boston: ©2007 City Maps, Inc

Index

Page numbers in **bold** indicate illustrations.

Paul Revere